Vegan Ventures

Start and Grow an Ethical Business

Also by Katrina Fox:

Why Compassion is Essential in Social Justice
(in *Circles of Compassion: Essays Connecting Issues of Justice*,
edited by Will Tuttle), Vegan Publishers, 2014

Vegan Journalist Blazing a Trail of Greater Awareness for All Beings
(in *Plant-Powered Women: Pioneering Vegan Female Leaders
Share Their Vision for a Healthier, Greener, Compassionate World*,
edited by Kathy Divine), CreateSpace, 2014

Trans People in Love (with Tracie O'Keefe), Routledge, 2008

Finding the Real Me: True Tales of Sex and Gender Diversity
(with Tracie O'Keefe), Jossey Bass, 2003

Trans-X-U-All: The Naked Difference (with Tracie O'Keefe),
Extraordinary People Press, 1997

Vegan Ventures

Start and Grow an Ethical Business

Katrina Fox

vegan**business**media

Dedicated to:

The change-makers who are creating a world in which all beings are free to thrive.

"May our daily choices be a reflection of our deepest values, and may we use our voices to speak for those who need us most, those who have no voice, those who have no choice."

— Colleen Patrick-Goudreau

Disclaimer:

This book is designed to provide general information on starting and running a vegan business only. This information is provided and sold with the knowledge that the publisher and author do not offer any legal, financial or other professional advice. In the case of a need for any such expertise, consult with the appropriate professional. This book does not contain all information available on the subject.

This book has not been created to be specific to any individuals' or organizations' situation or needs. Every effort has been made to make this book as accurate as possible. However, there may be typographical and/or content errors. Therefore, this book should serve only as a general guide and not as the ultimate source of subject information.

The examples stated in the book are not intended to represent or guarantee that anyone will achieve the same or similar results. Each individual's success depends on their background, dedication, desire and motivation. As with any business endeavor, there is an inherent risk of loss of capital and there is no guarantee that you will earn any money.

This book contains information that might be dated and is intended only to educate and entertain. The author and publisher shall have no liability or responsibility to any person or entity regarding any loss or damage incurred, or alleged to have incurred, directly or indirectly, by the information contained in this book.

Published by Vegan Business Media
An imprint of O'Keefe & Fox Industries Pty Ltd
Shop 3 Glebe Place, 131-145 Glebe Point Road, Glebe, NSW 2037, Australia
Email: info@veganbusinessmedia.com Website: www.veganbusinessmedia.com

International wholesale enquiries through Ingram.

Editing: Wayne Purdin
Cover design & text layout: Robin H. Ridley, Parfait Studio, www.parfaitstudio.com
Vegan Business Media logo: ThankTank Creative, www.thanktankcreative.com
Author headshot photo: John Donegan

ISBN: 978-0-9875109-0-7

Table of Contents

Acknowledgments

A book like this requires collaboration and support. The following people have provided that in spades on both a personal and professional level, and I'm deeply thankful:

My wife, Tracie O'Keefe, who has tirelessly supported and encouraged me in my writing and editing endeavors for nearly 25 years. Her resilience, compassion, and love have given me a foundation on which to thrive. She's the wind beneath my wings.

The 65 owners of the vegan-run businesses, PR, marketing, and business growth professionals who took time out of their busy schedules to answer my in-depth questions. Their generosity and honesty in sharing challenges and insights to help others succeed is humbling.

Philip Wollen for finding time in his packed schedule to write the foreword and for being a beacon of goodwill to people, animals, and planet through his wonderful work with the Kindness Trust.

Marcia 'Butterflies' Katz for her helpful blog posts listing vegan businesses across the globe, many of which are featured in this book.

Clare Mann and Brendan Norris from Communicate31 and *Ethical Futures* digital magazine for challenging me to get out of my comfort zone in relation to business and selling.

Voiceless: The Animal Protection Institute for awarding me the 2014 media prize for print/online journalism, an unexpected yet welcome recognition that spurred me on to write this book.

My best friend, Mandy, with whom I've shared some of the wildest adventures of my life, for always encouraging me to express my passions; in this case, writing this book.

Susan Paget for her encouragement and lived example of what's possible when you follow your passion.

Wayne Purdin for his editing skills.

Robin Ridley from Parfait Studio for her beautiful cover design and typesetting. Her attention to detail, 'can do' attitude and patience made her a pleasure to work with.

Melissa Stefano for her courage, boldness, trust, and willingness to share connections and resources with me.

My dear friend Georgina Abrahams for reminding me to get off the computer occasionally and connect to my spirituality and creativity.

Demetrius Bagley, *Vegucated* producer and business adviser, for his generous insights and support of this project.

Rach Moran for her loyal friendship, beautiful songs and for brainstorming book titles with me at 2am.

And Kay Holder, the woman who changed my life profoundly in 1996 by gently explaining the concept of veganism to me. Her compassionate, non-judgmental approach saw me embrace vegan living pretty much instantly.

Foreword

This book is a timely addition to the reading list of every vegan entrepreneur. Katrina Fox distills the essence of each contributor succinctly.

I have had some experience in the business world, in a number of industries, as a banker, corporate adviser, and owner, and I found myself subconsciously nodding in agreement as I read many of the book's recommendations.

People are drawn to veganism by a variety of forces: Animal cruelty, human health, greenhouse gas emissions, ocean acidification, water wastage, non-human animal rights, and non-violence generally. One quality they all share is their commitment to avoiding the use of animals for human purposes.

For people in the "vegan business" world, there are some encouraging trends. This is a market space that is growing rapidly. The world is becoming "veganized." It is no longer an easily dismissed niche market. It is now a global movement. For the start-up entrepreneur, it is an opportunity to capture a small share of a growing market, a delicious recipe for growth. For an established vegan business, it is a welcome refresher course.

Building an ethical business is a noble and exciting undertaking. The first objective of any business is to be profitable. The book corrects a belief amongst some ethical people that business is a zero-sum game, where making a profit means exploiting a customer, employee, or other stakeholder. The book takes the reader on a road trip, describing the rocky terrain of businesses generally, and vegan businesses in particular.

The future for well-run, properly structured, and strategically positioned vegan businesses has never been brighter. It is my hope that the next billionaire will set up a vegan version of McDonald's. My guess is that he or she will be from India, most likely from Gujarat.

I remember Ray Kroc, the founder of McDonald's, being quoted as telling his employees, "You will not succeed in this company unless you can see the beauty in a McDonald's bun." Well, I do understand the message that he was trying to impart. And I endorse the principle wholeheartedly. After all, it is axiomatic that successful business people must believe in their product. But I also say that civilization will not advance a jot until we see the cruelty, catastrophic health impacts, and environmental devastation in a meat-based burger.

Ethical vegans carry burdens and responsibilities that non-vegans do not.

Firstly, vegans are constantly aware, even subliminally, of the powerful reasons why they decided to enter this market niche. The sounds, smells, and images of the slaughterhouse; the razed forests; the poisoned oceans; the vivisection laboratories; the factory farms; the cruel dairies; and the leather tanneries are never far from their minds. All businesses are stressful. But these are additional stressors for vegans that non-vegan proprietors rarely experience in their unexamined lives.

Secondly, all businesses are subject to scrutiny, not just from statutory authorities, but also from their customers and suppliers. Nowhere is the scrutiny more intense than in the vegan community, which is a notoriously "hard marker." Every product, service, and ingredient in the supply chain will be scrutinized by fellow vegans to validate its vegan credentials. Vegans are justifiably hard on non-vegans for good reason, but are renowned for being harder on vegans who do not quite measure up to their subjective standards.

Thirdly, there is the complexity of failure. Most start-ups fail in their first year of operation, and many more in the first five years. When a non-vegan business fails, the loss is quarantined to the loss of capital, a future source of income, and the emotional angst of experiencing failure. But when a vegan business fails, the loss covers all the same elements but with an additional burden of having failed the animals, the vegan community, their own moral *raison d'être*, and ultimately, the vegan cause as well.

Finally, entrepreneurs who decide to promote their business under the "vegan" banner must recognize their responsibility to the vegan cause. When a business places a vegan decal or a sign on their building, they are morally obliged to treat every stakeholder with utmost integrity. If anyone is subsequently aggrieved by the actions of a vegan business, there are two things they will always remember: The name of the proprietor, and the fact that it was "vegan."

No wonder successful vegan entrepreneurs need to be made of hardy, sturdy, sterner stuff.

This book will also appeal to non-vegan business people who wish to add vegan choices to their range. In my experience, enterprises that do so will be opening the door to more vegan opportunities each year. In effect, they will be creating a new income stream with bigger profits destined for the bottom line.

I should stress that every business owner should have some financial accounting skills in their quiver. They should learn two lessons early: You cannot manage what you cannot measure. And "profit" (calculated by generally accepted accounting principles) is an opinion. Cash flow is a fact. Cash is no longer king. It is emperor.

Many years ago, I conducted a study of a range of companies, comparing the relative profitability of vegetarian and non-vegetarian businesses. They all shared similar general metrics: Revenue, head count, rents, overheads, and leverage (the ratio of debt to equity). The surprising conclusion was that the "veg" businesses achieved a return on equity double that of the "non-veg" businesses. The main reasons for this astonishing conclusion were threefold: Higher gross profit margins, less product wastage or spoilage, and more repeat business from "destination" customers.

I expect to see more vegan businesses drawing public attention to their inherent ethical qualities. Naturally, this should not simply be greenwash, but deeply ingrained codes of ethical behavior that resonate with the realities on the ground.

I have often asked owners of businesses that trade in animal products if they would allow their own children to do "work experience" in their businesses and also attend other interconnected businesses along their supply chain back to the factory farm and slaughterhouse. Very few of them agreed.

I also asked business executives a series of questions: What ethical policies would they establish if their family name were on the building? How would they respond if I showed them a way that guaranteed their name would never be on the front page of the newspaper alongside the words "cruelty," "fraud," "animal abuse," "negligence," or "crime"? If their business could be inoculated from ever having this disgrace, would the price earnings multiple of their shares increase or decrease? If the whole stock market knew that their company would never be disgraced on the front page of the newspaper, do you think it would encourage more investors or fewer investors? Would their bonds or bank debt be priced higher or lower? Would their shares trade at a premium or a discount to the industry? Would they attract more qualified or less qualified staff? And, by the way, who do you think is more ethical, *ceteris paribus* (all other things being equal): a vegan or a non-vegan?

Some years ago, I conducted an analysis of the most powerful global brand names in the world, covering banking, aviation, defense, manufacturing, insurance, chemicals, newspapers, education, television, agriculture, telecommunications, power generation, mining, central banks, cosmetics, food and beverages, and transport. They all had much in common.

These blue-chip companies were highly respected household names, each with high-powered boards, great political influence internationally, employing millions of people around the globe. Every one of them was also subjected to intense scrutiny from government authorities, auditors, external analysts, and the financial press. Apart from their Ivy League Boards of Directors and the gravitas and awe with which all these companies were perceived, they had another thing in common.

They were all convicted of massive crimes.

I prepared a long schedule, detailing their names, revenues, market capitalization, and then included the financial penalties imposed by the courts on them for their crimes. I commenced adding up these fines and penalties. Sheer exhaustion made me stop the exercise when the penalties went past one trillion dollars.

That is, USD $1,000,000,000,000.

It made me ponder how much more their market capitalization would have been if they had not engaged in such egregious criminal conduct in the first place?

It is clear that there is a dramatic disconnect between what some business owners claim to believe, and what they do in practice.

The "take away" message is simple: Ethics and profits are not mutually exclusive ideas. Anyone who claims to be a rational, responsible and respectable business person must see profits and ethics as two sides of the same coin.

I fervently believe that veganism is the engine of redirected economic growth. And small, agile, and ethical businesses are its fuel.

I am pleased that Katrina Fox has written this book.

It takes courage, tenacity, and energy to start and run a successful business. It takes integrity to also make it vegan. Vegans possess these qualities in abundance.

I look forward with great excitement to the day when it will no longer be necessary to describe a business or a person as "vegan." It will be a human trait as inspiring as entrepreneurship and a phenomenon as natural as breathing.

I cannot wait for that beautiful day to dawn.

Philip Wollen
Former Vice-President, Citibank
Founder, Winsome Constance Kindness Trust
(Venture Capital for Good Causes)
www.kindnesstrust.com

Introduction

I'll cut right to the chase. The mission of this book is Vegan World Domination—one business at a time.

I never thought I'd write a "business" book. My background is journalism (and before that, performing arts). I was a writer, an artist, a creative, and a champion of social justice for the oppressed and underdog.

From sit-down student protests in the late 1980s, being chased by riot police in fields during demonstrations against vivisection in the mid-1990s, to penning features and opinion pieces in niche and mainstream media for the past 17 years, calling for equality for marginalized people and animals, I was very much part of the activist movement, particularly animal rights.

For most of my life, I associated "business" with being stuffy, boring, conservative, bland, homogenized, conformist, greedy, and unethical. Money, I believed, was—as the cliché goes—the root of all evil, and hankering after it meant you were prepared to sell your soul to the corporate devil and allow yourself to be sucked into the immoral capitalist vortex that had no qualms about carrying out unspeakable atrocities by exploiting people, harming animals, and destroying the planet in its pursuit of profit at any cost.

It was no wonder that as soon as money came into my life, I was quick to send it on its way. After the Global Financial Crisis of 2008 and the massive changes impacting journalism, I started to reassess my career and life. I immersed myself in personal development trainings and a coaching course and started to put myself out as a media coach and trainer. I got some speaking gigs, mostly at events for small business owners and entrepreneurs. And, while I love teaching and training, I knew I had to find a niche and clientele I was passionate about and desired with all my heart to help succeed.

My epiphany came after I returned from a trip to New York and Los Angeles in 2012 and realized that vegan business owners and entrepreneurs were everywhere. They were in the restaurants where I ate in the US, my current home country Australia, and my original home town of London in the UK; the skincare and cosmetics companies I bought my potions, lotions, and screaming red lipstick from; the shoe companies that covered my feet in sensible walking shoes and platform heels; and the manufacturers of all the food stuffs I stocked my fridge and cupboards with.

The two words together "vegan business" suddenly gave the "business" part new meaning. I realized that owning and operating a vegan business is a form of animal rights activism. And helping vegan business owners and entrepreneurs succeed in starting and growing their enterprises is also a form of activism.

Talk about putting a different spin on something. It's called a *reframe*, and you'll find out more about it in the chapter on mindset.

The universe must have conspired because, toward the end of 2013, veganism was starting to be "on trend." Even *New York Magazine* reported that "news outlets on both sides of the Atlantic are already declaring 2014 'the year of the vegan'" (Rami, 2014). And, in just the first couple of months of 2015, vegan living was hitting the headlines regularly—in a positive way.

Vegan food was served at the British Academy of Film and Television Arts (BAFTA) Awards (Khomami, 2015). Vegan leather saw a spike in sales (Li, 2015). Pop star Beyoncé launched a plant-based eating delivery service (Lorenz, 2015). *Fortune* magazine ran an article on high-end, cruelty-free fashion (Guilmet, 2015). A vegan cheese company got a deal on the popular US reality TV show *Shark Tank* (Holland, 2014). UK newspaper

The Guardian reported on the rise of "vegepreneurs" (Clarkson, 2014. Beyond Meat (the food company that high-profile organizations and individuals, including Microsoft founder Bill Gates, have invested in), was featured on *The Today Show* where a group of people were asked to do a taste test between real chicken and beef and Beyond Meat chicken and beef. On both occasions, the taste testers believed the Beyond Meat products were the animal-based meat (Stump, 2014).

As Tim Barford, co-organizer of the hugely successful Veg-FestUK vegan lifestyle festivals, told me, the opportunities for people of all ages to start and grow vegan-run businesses are unprecedented:

"Our kids don't have any new music to listen to; we've done all that for them. There's no chance of discovering house music again, punk rock, or psychedelic electric blues—that's all been done," he said. "But with this whole vegan thing, suddenly there are generations of people, perhaps born in the '50s, '60s, '70s, and now, of course, younger, even in their teens and early 20s, who are able to pioneer whole businesses in this new, developing market."

For me, the question was: How could I, with my skills as a journalist, content creator and curator, interviewer and media coach/trainer launch my own business to help vegan business owners and entrepreneurs?

I knew there were a ton of general business books out there, many of them excellent for any small business owner starting up. But there was nothing specifically for the owners of vegan-run businesses. While many of the challenges, advice, and strategies apply to any business, running an animal-free operation brings its own set of extra, specific challenges.

So, I wrote this book because I wanted to read it.

In addition to reading more general business books, including the wonderful *Shark Tank: Jump Start Your Business* by author and entrepreneur Michael Parish Dudell—which I highly recommend you read in conjunction with this one—I wanted to find out from vegan business owners and entrepreneurs themselves what their secrets of success were. How did they cope with the challenges of running an ethical business? What did they learn? How did they grow?

Thus began this book project. I interviewed 65 owners of vegan-run businesses in the US, Canada, UK, and Australia, along with vegan marketing, PR, and business growth professionals.

The main criterion was that they had run their business/es for at least five years. (Victoria Moran's Main Street Vegan Academy had been in operation for three years at the time of our interview, but she has been in business as an *Oprah*-featured author and speaker, often about vegan topics, for over 25 years.)

Some of the vegan-run businesses whose owners I interviewed have been around for decades. Plamil Foods in the UK, for example, was formed in the 1960s. Other businesses started up more recently, within the past five years, and the rest began anywhere in between. The majority I spoke with provided products, including food, skincare, and fashion, and a few provided services.

Many of the businesses also factor in, as much as possible, human rights and sustainability in regards to their offerings, recognizing that veganism is about compassion for *all* beings.

As you go through the book, which is filled with nuggets of wisdom from these passionate and hardworking entrepreneurial change-makers, you'll see that, while there are some common threads, there's no one-size-fits-all advice or strategies. Sometimes, you'll read conflicting advice from different people. The aim of this book is to equip you with knowledge so you can make informed choices that suit you and your business.

You won't get it right all the time. You will make mistakes, which, while not pleasant at the time, are part of your learning curve, growth, and path to success. But wherever you are on your journey—perhaps you have an idea to start a business, are in the early stages of development, or are in the throes of expanding your empire—I hope you'll be educated and inspired by your fellow vegan business owners and entrepreneurs who took valuable time out of their schedules to answer my extensive questions and share their expertise with you.

As I mentioned earlier, there are plenty of general business books out there, and I recommend you read them (there's a small list at the back of this book in the Resources section). While much of the advice is applicable to most businesses, this is the first book, as far as I'm aware, to focus specifically on vegan-run businesses, the particular challenges they face, and how they deal with them to succeed and grow.

Each of the 10 chapters follows a successive flow, building on the content from the previous chapter.

Chapter 1 begins with the *why*. If your reason, your purpose for running your business, isn't strong enough, it's unlikely to succeed; so being clear on this is crucial.

Chapter 2 is about mindset. If you don't have a mindset for success, or have issues around money and business, you'll likely sabotage your ventures.

Chapter 3 looks at the structuring and setting up of your business and the importance of systems.

Chapter 4 demonstrates how the quality of our relationships is key to the success of our businesses.

In Chapter 5, we discuss branding while Chapters 6 to 10 focus on marketing and PR.

The Afterword rounds off the book with vegan business owners and entrepreneurs sharing the main lessons they have learned through running their operations.

After the Resources section, there's a list of all the vegan business owners and entrepreneurs who graciously granted me an interview—about half were done via email, the rest by phone or Skype. I encourage you to check out their websites, support them, and connect with them via social media.

Finally, as the book progressed, I found I couldn't fit everything into it because the interviewees were so generous with their insights. So, in March, 2015, I launched the Vegan Business Media website (**www.veganbusinessmedia.com**). Throughout the book, you'll find links to various tools, articles and templates on the site. They're free, so I recommend you take advantage and download them.

I wish you every success in starting and/or growing your vegan-run business. Like you, I want to live in a world where we can walk along the main street, in a shopping mall, or at the airport and every business is run on vegan principles.

Yes, I know it sounds idealistic, but if we don't dream it and aim for it, it won't happen. We, as vegan business owners and entrepreneurs, are at the forefront of planting the seeds of change. Go make it happen.

Katrina Fox
August, 2015

Chapter 1

Define Your Purpose

Start with the "why" and the "how" will take care of itself. That's the advice of some business gurus. It's actually not quite that simple. The *how* of running a business doesn't just happen by itself; it takes planning, strategy, and a lot of work.

But you do need to start with the *why*—the higher purpose or ideal behind your business.

In his TED talk, *How Great Leaders Inspire Action,* Simon Sinek, author of *Start With Why,* explains the concept of the Golden Circle in business: The outer circle is the *What,* the middle circle is the *How,* and the inner circle is the *Why.*

"Every person, every single organization on the planet knows WHAT they do, 100 percent. Some know HOW they do it, whether you call it your differentiating value proposition or your proprietary process or your USP [unique selling proposition]. But very, very few people and organizations know WHY they do what they do" (Sinek, 2009).

And if you're thinking your "why" is to make money, think again, says Sinek, who argues that profit is a given result. The *why* is the purpose, the cause, the belief underpinning your business. It's the reason your business exists; it's why you get out of bed in the morning, and it's why anyone should care.

Most businesses focus their marketing efforts on telling people what they offer and how they're different or better, says Sinek. For example, a car manufacturer proclaims, "This is our new car and here's why it's cool. Would you like to buy one?" If Apple followed this model, its marketing would be along the lines of, "We make computers and they're designed beautifully.

Would you like to buy one?" Not particularly inspiring.

What Apple actually does is start with the *why*, Sinek explains. The company's marketing message is, "We believe in challenging the status quo and thinking differently; we do this by making our products beautifully designed, simple to use, and user-friendly. We just happen to make computers. Would you like to buy one?"

See the difference? The famous *1984* commercial that introduced the Macintosh personal computer didn't show a single computer, except for a stylized image of an Apple computer on the heroine's shirt, but it got the message (saving humanity from conformity) across powerfully.

All successful organizations, regardless of their size, start with and communicate their *why* to their employees and to their customers, says Sinek. They inspire, rather than manipulate people into taking action. Staff who are inspired by their leaders (as we will see in Chapter 4 on relationships) are your biggest advocates, as opposed to those who follow your rules through force. The same goes for customers. They're far more likely to spread the word about your products or services if they're impassioned by your business's purpose.

Having a purpose for your business is a motivator to stick with it and do your utmost to ensure its success. I'm not saying that money and profit aren't important—far from it—as without either of these, you'll quickly go out of business, which helps no one. But if you're in it solely for the money, the chances are that when the going gets tough or when you find yourself doing tasks you dislike, you're more likely to quit.

When your mission, cause, or purpose is bigger than you and something you're so committed to in mind, body, and soul, you'll love that business like it's your baby (baby animal if human children aren't your thing!). On the days when everything goes wrong and you're on the verge of a meltdown or tears and your stress levels go through the roof, you come back to your *why*.

You take a deep breath and feel your mind, body, and spirit re-energized to carry on because you know, with all your heart, that this is your calling.

When you're doing what you're meant to, you become willing to learn new skills, meet new people, and be pushed out of your comfort zone. When you're on purpose with a cause or mission you're passionate about, "work" becomes a pleasure (this doesn't mean every day is always hunky dory with no challenges; it means that you are inspired to keep going).

Business for Animal Rights
For the owners of many vegan-run businesses, animal rights or welfare is front and center of their mission. Operating a vegan-run business is a form of activism that helps animals by encouraging people to make kinder, compassionate choices.

One of the longest-running vegan businesses is Plamil Foods in the UK, which manufactures a range of products, including milk alternatives and chocolate. The company was started by a group of individuals, committed to bringing dairy-free milk to the public, shortly after Donald Watson founded The Vegan Society in 1944. One of the group was the late Arthur Ling, already a pioneer in sustainability through his bio-fuels business that produced sunflower oils for farmers' tractors.

His son and Plamil Foods's managing director Adrian Ling explains:

"One of the first meetings of The Vegan Society back in the 1940s was to look at ways of having a dairy-free milk. A committee formed to look into producing it. After the war, people were moving around the country and committees are by their very nature long-winded sometimes. So this group of people, including my father, spent over 10 years discussing the ways they were going to go about doing it.

"Towards the late 1950s, the group formed the Plant-Milk Society, which again became a bit of a chatting box until the early

1960s when they formed a limited company by the same name. Around 1964 they decided to actually produce a milk. After spending a considerable amount of money on research into leaf proteins, they settled on soya and produced the first soya milk.

"As the company continued to grow and branch out into other food items, it changed its name to Plamil, which is made up of the first three letters of the words *plant* and *milk*, in 1972," says Ling.

I've been a fan of Plamil chocolate since 1996 when I became vegan and there were few animal-free chocolate options. Yet, even now, while there are a smorgasbord of vegan chocolates available, I'll still grab a Plamil bar because of its inspiring history and continuing mission to create vegan food products in a dedicated manufacturing facility free from animal ingredients.

Animal activism was cited as the "why" for many of the other business owners interviewed for this book.

"I created the company to speak for animal rights and planet Earth and to support myself working on a mission larger than myself," says Elizabeth Olsen, owner of Olsenhaus vegan shoe brand in New York.

"My business is vegan because I am, because I refuse to be responsible for the suffering of animals, to the best of my knowledge and ability," says Tracy Perkins from skincare line Strawberry Hedgehog in Phoenix, Arizona. "It was tough at first to find vegan products so it makes what I do that much more rewarding, knowing that I am creating a pure product that like-minded people can enjoy, guilt-free."

"The why has always been—and always will be—for the animals," says Donna Oakes-Jones from Cow Jones Industrials, an online fashion boutique based in New York. "I've been a vegan since 1989. In the beginning, I was very active with different organizations, leafleting, doing outreach, taking part in protests. The business is an extension of this activism."

"Understanding the horrors of the meat and dairy industry

is very upsetting and I was tired of just wallowing in sadness," says California-based Ilsa Hess, creator of Nacheez, a vegan nacho cheese. "I wanted to be part of a solution and give people an option to help them get away from animal-based dairy."

"The number-one reason is animal welfare; it tops the list," says Georgie Campbell, co-owner of Addiction Food, a range of vegan sweet treats in Australia. "We have fallen into the 'health food' movement, being plant-based and gluten-free, and that's great. But number one, first and foremost, is animal welfare and, basically, compassion for all living creatures. From this, our products were developed."

Image consultant Ginger Burr from Massachusetts had been running a successful business for 18 years before acknowledging the inherent cruelty in the fashion and beauty products she was recommending to her clients. She faced the task of changing her business to operate on vegan principles and risked losing potential and existing clients. Yet her "why" made it a no-brainer.

"I can't *not* do it. If I didn't share what I know and help people become more aware, like I wish someone had done for me 20 years earlier, then I'm consciously turning a blind eye to the needless suffering of animals, and I can't bear to do that," says Burr. "People expect that it's much harder to be vegan than it really is. This is only because it's *still* a foreign concept. Our world revolves around meat and dairy consumption and the wearing of wool and leather. It's so second nature that most people don't question it and can't imagine what their options would be if they didn't consume those products. My job is to create a new awareness and a realization that it's not only doable but pleasurable, and the rewards are not only in how the person looks or what they eat but also in how their heart feels."

Challenging Vegan Stereotypes
A desire to obliterate the image of veganism as boring, bland, unexciting, plain, and all the other negative associations lumped

on us fuelled the purpose of other interviewees into starting their businesses.

"The vegan world can seem, to an outsider, to be all about deprivation and strict rules," says Lagusta Yearwood, owner of Lagusta's Luscious, a hand-made chocolate line based in New York. "I like the idea of making vegan chocolate because it's so rich and luxurious. It shows people that veganism, even though it begins with a moral impulse, can be just as sophisticated and decadent as the mainstream food world."

"There are people who are making either a dietary transition from being omnivorous to vegetarian or vegan for ethical or health reasons, and, for both of those groups, I felt like there wasn't enough awesome, decadent food," says Ella Nemcova, owner of New York-based The Regal Vegan, which manufactures Faux Gras. "There were plenty of burgers, macaroons, and other stuff, but there was nothing that was really naughty!"

"Rubyfruit was born in an effort to demonstrate that vegan food can be delicious, indulgent, and satisfying. It's our activism; if we can show people that vegan food can be wonderful, they're more likely to be receptive to the idea of a vegan lifestyle," says Amanda Solomons, co-owner of Rubyfruit café in the Blue Mountains near Sydney, Australia. "We believe people are inherently kind; they resist veganism partly due to convention and partly due to an inability to imagine what a vegan diet would look like. If they can imagine it, they assume it to be bland and boring, lacking in flavor, substance, and variety. We demonstrate otherwise."

Swami Hennessy-Mitchell, owner of CocoLuscious, a coconut milk ice cream line in Australia, dreams of "waking up on a vegan planet" and believes the best way to do this is to manufacture vegan products. "For many people, the hardest things to give up when becoming vegan are chocolate, ice cream, and cheese. I've covered the chocolate and ice cream, and have plans to do a vegan cheese some day," she says.

"Selfish" Motives

For other business owners, their "why" is a combination of concerns about animal exploitation along with "selfish" motives of making products or services available that they themselves can take advantage of. (I put the word *selfish* in quote marks because, of course, these business owners are providing a worthy service to many more people, not just themselves.)

Take Wally Fry, founder of Fry's Family Foods, which manufactures vegan meat alternatives that are available in more than 12,000 retail outlets internationally.

The company was started in 1992 in South Africa when Fry—a former livestock agent who sold cattle for slaughter—had an epiphany after being influenced by his vegetarian wife and being asked some pointed questions about animals by his then four-year-old daughter Tammy (now the company's marketing director).

"I realized there's a tremendous amount of environmental degradation taking place on our planet due to intensive animal or livestock farming. The more I looked into it, the more I saw the cruelty that was being meted out to these animals; so I decided that I wouldn't be part of or support the meat industry. That was my first decision," says Fry, whose business is now headquartered in Australia.

"But then the second decision was to become a vegetarian, which I found quite difficult. I missed having meat or protein on my plate, which, in a vegetarian meal, is usually loaded heavily on the side of carbohydrates. I knew that, unless I developed something for myself to eat to start off with, I might fail on the vegetarian front and find myself tempted back into the habit of eating meat.

"So I passionately and enthusiastically set about researching and developing a unique process of making this plant-based protein food, always with the constant view in mind that if successful, I would be able to help millions of other people who

34

have a similar consciousness about this issue and who want to become vegetarians or vegans but find it extremely difficult. In doing so, I would reduce meat eating and help reduce livestock farming in my own small way," says Fry.

Jeremy Johnson, founder of Vegan Perfection, a predominantly wholesale business supplying vegan goods to retailers in Australia, began the company with similar self-interest to begin with when he was unable to buy the range of vegan products he had become used to while living in the UK.

"I found that Australia was lacking good vegan food products, so I guess there was probably a partly selfish motive that got me started, with the aim of rectifying that lack," says Johnson.

Since those early days in 2006, his "why" has evolved: "We want to cater to vegans and give vegans access to good quality products, but we also want to show people that you can live an indulgent lifestyle as a vegan, while still adhering to your own moral code," says Johnson.

Sugandh G. Agrawal, founder and creator of GUNAS handbags in New York, found herself with a similar dilemma when she was unable to find high-quality, mid-priced, animal-free handbags.

"I love animals and I love fashion, but when I went out shopping, all I could find were brands where the price points and styles were extreme," says Agrawal. "There was nothing that filled the gap in the market, and I felt if I want something like that, I'm sure there are many people out there who want a bag that falls in that mid-priced category but is high fashion, high style, and doesn't compromise their values."

The Business of Health

Some owners of vegan-run businesses start out with a passion to inspire people to good health and eating a plant-based diet. Many, through their resulting association with the ethical vegan community, become aware of the atrocities involved in animal agriculture and animal exploitation in general and become ethical vegans.

Vegan health practitioners, whose clients are predominantly non-vegans, encourage plant-based eating as part of their mission to bring people to higher-quality levels of health, which also benefits animals and the planet.

"I want as many people to eat as many plant-based foods as I can. So the big motivator for me is to not just help people with their health but also help animals and help the environment," says California-based acupuncturist and Chinese Medicine practitioner Heather Lounsbury. "The more I can get my patients to go at least closer to plant-based, the better off they are."

"As someone trained in science, it's clear to me that an earth without diversity of species and animals is a poorer-quality place to live," says Dr Tracie O'Keefe, clinical hypnotherapist, naturopath, and business mindset coach in Sydney, Australia. "I'd like to think that those people who come after me have the chance to enjoy nature as much as I have. My business teaches people to live a vegan lifestyle for health, wellbeing, and good business practices. I see the use of animals as unnecessary for a modern, informed lifestyle, ethically unsound, and environmentally destructive."

While the large fast-food companies have established outlets nationally and internationally, Veggie Grill is hot on their trails. The vegan-run chain with an extensive menu of healthy, veggie dishes, has 28 restaurants in the US, in California, Oregon, and Washington at the time of writing.

"We started Veggie Grill because we were passionate about three things: the need for delicious, convenient, healthy food; the opportunity to show people how delicious veggie-centric foods could be; and the belief in the benefits of plant-centric food," explains co-founder T.K. Pillan.

Pillan's views are shared by other vegan restaurant owners, including Ben Asamani, owner and chef at 222 Veggie Vegan in

London; Ken Israel, owner of the Iku Wholefood brand in Sydney, Australia; Kendall Hayes, owner of two Iku franchises; and Joy Pierson and Bart Potenza from Candle Cafe, Candle Cafe West and Candle 79 in New York.

Pierson was a nutritional counselor in 1987 when she frequented Potenza's juice bar as a customer. A passion for health saw the couple embrace not only vegan but also organic, ethical, and sustainable principles in their Candle enterprises.

It's this passion and the feedback from clients that has been the driving force and motivation behind the three outlets over the past 28 years. Their purpose goes far beyond simply running a restaurant business.

"We had a customer who we didn't know was eating here every day after doing chemotherapy. After she passed away, one of her friends came in with a dozen yellow roses and said we brightened up her life so much. She just wanted us to know that," says Pierson. "That keeps me going because if you can make somebody's life brighter and better, with brilliant food that's fresh from the farm, with no violence and no anger, it's really amazing. What a gift! For everybody. I would never do this if it was 'just a restaurant.' It would never be the business choice that I would make."

While Israel, Potenza, and Pierson are long-time pioneers of the healthy, plant-based, wholefood movement, Whitney Lauritsen, aka Eco-Vegan Gal of the ecovegangal.com website, is among a group of more recent entrepreneurs, spreading the messages of health, compassion to all beings, and sustainability. California-based Lauritsen, who's "passionate about inspiring, educating, and empowering people to lead the healthiest, happiest lives possible," creates multimedia content and products to this end. "The more savvy I am with Eco-Vegan Gal, the more people I can reach, so it's really motivating to take the business side of things seriously," she says.

People, Animals, Planet

Veganism is about rejecting animal exploitation and products or services that use animal-based ingredients wherever possible. But for many people, it's an ideology that must also incorporate humans and the planet in its quest for compassion for all beings. Many of the business owners interviewed for this book also factor human rights and sustainability into their operations, while others are working toward this.

"Our main mission is to create delicious vegan foods for people's health, the health of the planet, and the health of the animals, farm animals, in particular, that are very abused," says Seth Tibbott, founder of Turtle Island Foods, makers of the renowned Tofurky line of products.

Kevin Newell, owner of Humane Wildlife Solutions in the UK, saw an opportunity to help people, animals, and planet by filling a gap in the market for non-lethal pest control. "I wanted to do a job that would be rewarding, a job I loved, and it was simply not there in the market. At the same time, I wanted to help animals. After reading about how many urban foxes in the UK were killed each year by the pest control industry, I wondered why there was no one helping them," says Newell. "In the British countryside, foxes are hunted weekly, and the foxes are aided by hunt saboteurs, but in the cities, where thousands of foxes are killed every year, there was apparently no help for them at all. There simply was no non-lethal alternative to pest control out there. So I decided that I would offer this service and give the wildlife in the cities of the UK a chance for life and the people a non-lethal alternative to their wildlife problems."

Melissa Dion, founder and owner of Ecolissa, an online ethical fashion retailer based in Massachusetts, is driven by the desire to support brands that share her values, including vegan, fair trade, and environmentally sustainable. "I've worked for a number of different companies in the past and have learned that it's important to agree with and believe in the ethics of the organization you work for. What better way to do this than to start your own business?"

Your "Why" May Evolve

As we noted earlier, Vegan Perfection's Jeremy Johnson saw his "why" change from catering solely to the needs of vegans to educating a wider audience about veganism.

Jessica Bailey, owner of The Cruelty Free Shop in the Australian cities of Sydney and Melbourne, had a similar experience of her purpose expanding. Bailey started her business online in 2001 and built up a loyal clientele of vegan customers. When she opened her first physical shop in Sydney in 2012, she initially expected to service a similar clientele.

But while the local vegan community do frequent the shop, Bailey's drivers behind the business have expanded into "public education" around veganism and animal rights issues. This takes the form of alternating the shop frontage windows with vegan products and animal rights campaigns.

"Our mission has gone from providing a service to the vegan community to helping to make it easier to be vegan. It's become more about delivering a message to the broader community rather than a subset of the community," says Bailey.

What is Your "Why"?

If you're already operating a vegan-run business, your "why" may be clear—but it doesn't hurt to revisit it and ensure that, if it has evolved, you're communicating this clearly to your customers and clients on your website and other marketing materials.

If you're considering starting a vegan-run business or are in the start-up stage, get your purpose down now. Take some time out in a quiet place alone, close your eyes and take five to 10 slow, deep breaths. Ask yourself:

What is my number-one reason for starting my business and running it on vegan principles? (Trust the answer that comes up first; don't censor yourself and do be honest.)

What are other reasons for starting my business and running it on vegan principles? (Again, be honest.)

Is my reason, my "why" big enough to get me out of bed each morning, looking forward to the day?

Why is it so important to me to start this business and operate it ethically?

Open your eyes and write down what came up for you (even if some of your answers made you feel uncomfortable).

Ego vs. Higher Ideals

Chances are, if you're like most people, some of your answers may have been in your own interest. Perhaps you want a particular lifestyle that involves fancy holidays or high-end clothes; you may want to become known as an ethical entrepreneur or the Richard Branson of the vegan business community; or you like the idea of being in charge.

None of these kinds of answers are wrong. Some business coaches argue that if you make it all about you, you're not able to serve your target market properly. While that certainly has some truth to it, it's also true that we need to be authentic, otherwise our target market (and anyone else) will smell the incongruency, which leads to distrust.

We are people, and humans are complicated. We have, what Debbie Ford encapsulates in her books on the subject, a shadow side to us. Our shadow is those things we'd rather not think about ourselves or have other people know about us. Rather than rejecting or suppressing our shadow qualities, which simply lends strength to them, we need to acknowledge, embrace, and integrate them into our lives so they can serve us—and others—constructively.

We all have egos, and it's okay to desire recognition, as long as that's not the sole reason for starting your business. If it is, it probably stems from a feeling—conscious or unconscious—of not being good enough, and you'll likely expend an excessive amount of energy trying to prove your worth, which is exhausting. By learning to value and love yourself, you can channel your energy into building a successful and sustainable business whose foundation is to help others, and, by helping others, you help yourself.

We'll cover more about mindset and managing ourselves in Chapter 2, but, for now, focus on getting crystal clear on your "why."

Chapter 2
Mindset

Not everyone is cut out to be an entrepreneur or has what it takes to run a business. As we saw in the previous chapter, having a strong enough reason or higher purpose is essential for a business's success. Another key to your success (or otherwise) is your mindset.

If you're thinking this sounds a bit "woo woo" and are tempted to skip this chapter, I encourage you to stick with it because it's not always economic conditions that cause a business to fail—it's the mindset of the business owner.

Beliefs

Are you sabotaging yourself with your beliefs?

We all have conscious beliefs—that is, beliefs we're aware of (for example, as vegans, we believe that animals shouldn't be exploited or harmed). But we also have unconscious beliefs—inner self-talk that's going on out of our conscious awareness.

Much of the time, we're not aware of our unconscious beliefs, which is what can make them so dangerous.

Depending on what our conscious and unconscious beliefs are, we have the power to talk ourselves out of success—or into it. Our thinking has the power to sabotage or empower us.

Consciously, we may say we want our business to turn a profit, but if we have unconscious beliefs about money—such as it's evil or we don't deserve it—we'll develop strategies (often equally as unconscious) to ensure money doesn't flow easily to us. One part of us is saying, "Come hither" to money, but the hidden, more powerful part is saying, "Go away!"

"Mindset will be what holds you up in the long term when your buttons get pushed and you feel anxious and are wondering where the money is going to come from," says Sydney-based vegan psychologist Clare Mann. "Many people have a scarcity consciousness. When you do what you love, provide excellent service and solutions to people's problems, the money will follow. But you'll only earn as much or be as successful as you believe you're capable of."

If you have any doubts about the power of our beliefs, think about the placebo effect. People who are given what they believe to be a pain killer (but is not) experience their pain disappearing.

A belief is a feeling of certainty about something. Often, these beliefs are generalized. They're what personal development guru Anthony Robbins calls "global beliefs." They usually take the form of grand, sweeping statements such as "Life is …." Or "Relationships are …." Or "Vegans are …."

How we experience life, relationships, vegans, or anything else will depend on whether the beliefs we have about them are positive or negative. If you believe life is meant to be a hard struggle full of bitter disappointments, you'll experience it differently than someone who believes life is a wonderful adventure full of exciting challenges.

Our beliefs even cause our brains to change. They form what are called neural pathways. Imagine if, every day, you kept walking along the exact grassy path in a woodland. Eventually, it would be so worn that you'd carve out a dirt track. This is what beliefs do in our brains.

Our negative beliefs are generally caused by our (mis) interpretations of past events in our life that we attribute meaning to, usually born out of the three universal fears (False Evidence Appearing Real):

- Fear of not being loved or lovable
- Fear of not being (good) enough
- Fear of not belonging

"If you don't manage those self-destructive beliefs, all the passion, perseverance, and training in the world can't make up for it," warns image consultant Ginger Burr.

What Are Your Beliefs?

Take a few moments to discover what some of your beliefs are. You may be surprised!

Grab a piece of paper or notebook. Write down your answers to the following (write as many words for each as come up for you. Spend five minutes on each and let your answers flow by writing non-stop):

Life is _____

_____

Money is _____

_____

Business is _____

_____

Relationships are _____

_____

Success is _____

_____

People are _____

_____

I am _____

_____

Now, take a look at each of your answers and ask yourself: Is this belief serving me or hindering me? And if it's not serving you, what could you replace it with?

Yes, fortunately, we can change our beliefs and rewire those neural pathways in our brains. We can replace negative beliefs and thinking with positive and empowering beliefs and thought processes.

"In business, you must be a positive thinker and approach your business in a constructive way, each and every day," says vegan hypnotherapist, naturopath, and business mindset coach Dr Tracie O'Keefe. "There are days in your business when things seem to be going wrong, and those negative voices will come into your mind: 'This week is slow ... the economy isn't going well ... the rent is too high ... I'm useless ... why did I ever think I could succeed running my own business?' And so on. If those kinds of thoughts keep occurring, you'll end up miserable and stressed. By reprogramming your mind through techniques such as hypnosis, you can feel energized, motivated, and solution-focused."

Money Mindset

Many ethical business owners, including vegans, have major issues around money. Perhaps it's because many of us come from an activist background where valuing money means you're greedy and the "enemy" of all that's good. Or, you may be a creative—an artist, writer, designer, photographer—and believe that being broke is a badge of honor, indicating that you're the "real deal" while those raking in the dough are "sell-outs."

Victoria Moran, author and owner of vegan lifestyle coaching program Main Street Vegan Academy, has this advice:

"Many of us as vegans are drawn to a simple life and non-material values, and yet, the more money we have, the more we can help the animals. I get appeals, as we all do, and want to contribute to all of them, ideally enough to make a difference. Of course we all give in a variety of ways, and I'm grateful that

I contribute by writing books, giving lectures, and sending my Main Street Vegan Academy graduates out into the world to coach, teach and carry the message. Still, I look forward to the day when I'll be able to contribute more in a financial way, too," says Moran, before recounting the story of a woman she once knew who was "extremely wealthy."

"She moved in very big New York City circles of wealth, and one day she said to me, 'You might think you know what it is to have fun in life, but until you can give money away you don't know what it is to have fun.' I'm sure she's right, because even donating at a modest level gives me a great deal of joy. It pushes me to remind my students, as they're thinking about their pricing or about invoicing, that getting paid is essential for them to be of help to the animals. I know it's difficult to go to somebody who owes you money and say, 'Okay, it's time to pay.' It's like, 'Oh my gosh! I can't do that!' But you have to do that because your business has to keep its doors open so that you can help the animals directly. You need to prosper so that you can help in every possible way."

What Moran has done is to reframe how to think about earning and chasing up money. Reframing means taking a concept, experience, or belief and putting a different spin on it. As I described in the Introduction, once I reframed running a vegan business as a form of animal rights activism, it was so much easier to embrace it.

Tim Barford, owner of Yaoh hemp products and co-organizer of VegFestUK, says it's crucial to like doing business and be willing to be flexible in your operations. "If money's a dirty word for you, it's possibly not a great idea to set up a business. Are you going to be able to live with the compromises that you might have to make? So, on the one hand, it might be a really good idea to do something or to take that approach, but, on the other hand, it might have a contradiction in another part of your business, especially if you're an ethical business. You've got to

46

make decisions. Are you flexible enough? Do you actually care about your ethics enough? Do you care about them too much? Either can be an issue."

In addition to loving business and making money, you must also learn to love marketing and selling. While dodgy and desperate sales people have given these words a bad rap in their efforts to foist their wares upon us when we have no interest in them, psychologist Clare Mann offers a reframed perspective:

"Marketing is sharing your love of your product or service with those who are eagerly seeking your solution to their problems. Selling is the exchange of goods or services so the customer's problems are solved, their needs are met, and the business owner has the opportunity to ethically solve their problems and know they have sold them something that will positively improve their lives," says Mann.

Jessica Burman, owner of Cocoon Apothecary, a natural skincare line in Canada, has learned to embrace a 'selling' mindset. "The focus, once you're up and running, should be sales, sales, sales. It's all about the hustle. You need money or you won't survive. Being an ethical company doesn't mean you follow different rules. You have to work for sales like every other company," says Burman.

Embracing a positive mindset around money means valuing yourself and your products or services. Many vegan business owners, particularly when starting out, devalue their worth or feel guilty about charging their prices. This attitude serves no one, including animals.

"Since no customer can ever believe in you if you don't believe in yourself, a successful business owner must believe that their business creates tremendous value," says David Benzaquen, CEO of New York-based marketing consultancy PlantBased Solutions. "This is very easily reflected in the quality of salesmanship, as no person can ever inspire someone about a business offering more than the passionate founder or owner. If you can't do it, who will?"

The Cruelty Free Shop's Jessica Bailey was given a sharp reminder by a local government business mentor of the need to let go of her money mindset limitations.

"It was at a point where the business was stagnating a little bit and I wasn't quite sure how to take the next step. So, I had a couple of sessions with this guy," she explains. "He helped me look at the business in a different way, and the main thing he said to me was, 'You're not a charity. You actually need to make money, not for yourself, but to keep the business functioning, so you need to toughen up and put your margins up.'

"And I said, 'Oh no, I can't do that; I don't want to rip people off!' He replied, 'Well, if you're not here in a year's time, what use are you to anybody?' So I put all my margins up, and the direct result of that is we're still here today because, otherwise, we would have had to close the doors," says Bailey.

Entrepreneur Mindset
In addition to cultivating a successful money mindset, you also need to develop the mindset of an entrepreneur and business owner, as opposed to that of an employee.

"Write down your goals every day, and tell yourself that you will achieve these business goals," says Australian speaker and executive coach Ron Prasad. "You cannot have a business and have the mindset of an employee. I remember I was coaching a small business in 2012. The director of that company wanted to offer shares in the business to his general manager. After some coaching, he decided against doing that because he realized the general manager had an employee mentality and wouldn't succeed as a business partner. You must think like an entrepreneur, act like one, and picture yourself being one now."

We'll look more at the differences between an entrepreneur, employee and manager in the next chapter.

Qualities Needed to Run a Business

Let's take a look at some of the qualities you need to develop to run a business if you don't already have them.

Out of the interviews I did with the 65 owners of vegan-run businesses for this book, these were the qualities that were cited the most, starting with the most frequently mentioned:

- Resilience
- Patience
- Courage
- Flexibility
- Adaptability
- Drive
- Determination
- Self-Discipline
- Commitment
- Strong work ethic
- Belief
- Passion
- Risk taking
- Sense of humor
- Good communication skills
- Leadership, including self
- Teamwork
- Humility
- Open-mindedness
- Confidence
- Assertiveness
- Motivation
- Dedication
- Focus

The majority of interviewees stressed the importance of personal development when running a business and being an entrepreneur. It's not all about being touchy-feely; it's about managing yourself and your communication with staff and customers, both offline and online. As most of us have no doubt seen, it's all too easy to get angry, lash out, and damage your reputation as well as that of your brand.

Being able to manage your emotions is also a good motivator and prevents you from giving up when the going gets tough.

100 Percent Commitment

The Regal Vegan's Ella Nemcova says running and growing any business requires that you have the desire to persevere despite your ego.

"You have to be able to be a little like an athlete at some level, because it can be very painful to fall off the bike. You have to be able to keep getting up every time you're knocked down, like a boxer. If you don't get up, the game is over."

A positive "can do" attitude and a "100 percent commitment" is what Georgie Campbell attributes to the success of Addiction Food.

"I've got a *crazy* passion with a 'can do' attitude and, sometimes, it's just so full-on and I just look and I laugh and I think the difference between actually making it or not getting there is you've got to have 100 percent commitment; not 95 percent, not 98 percent; you've got to be 100 percent committed to your mission. Nothing else can come into it. You can't go, 'Maybe we'll see how it goes.' It's all or nothing, because you don't just want to buy yourself a job, you want to run the business," says Campbell.

Campbell adds that business owners must be prepared to do everything themselves, multitask, and be experts at it, particularly in the beginning if cash flow is in short supply. Her philosophy is shared by Candle restaurant chain owners Joy Pierson and Bart Potenza.

"Bart and I have a 'no matter what' kind of attitude," says Pierson. "So if we have to go in and clean, we do it. Like during a hurricane, we had to go in and prep the vegetables because we didn't want to bring in staff. I clean the bathroom whenever I am there too. I think of the restaurants like my home."

Failure is Not an Option

There's a lot of buzz in the entrepreneurial world about the importance of failure and the need to fail so you can learn and grow. This is true. But sometimes, failure can be a luxury that some business owners can't afford, which drives their determination for success. In Seth Tibbott's case, necessity kept him motivated for nearly 20 years with his struggling tempeh business before hitting the big time with Tofurky.

"I think that our business worked because it *had* to work. I didn't have a fall-back option," he says. "I moved up here an hour and a half from Portland into the middle of the woods with this tempeh business, and I don't know what I would've done if that had collapsed.

"A friend of mine started a vegan cheese business *years* ago. Right now vegan cheese is a hot, supercharged category; it's expanding. He was one of the first ones. He had a great product, a great idea, but he was an ex child actor on American television and he had money coming in from that. So he would say, 'Oh, I'm not going to make cheese right now; I'm going to go to Japan for a month, I'll make more when I come back.' It didn't *have* to work for him.

"You have to say, 'I'm going to make this work. I'm just totally committed.' Most people would say, 'Twenty years and you're not making money? Have you ever thought that maybe you're doing the wrong thing?' But I never really seriously considered *not* doing it," says Tibbott.

Colorado-based author and vegan lifestyle coach JL Fields agrees.

"How much money do you need to make in order to pay your rent or your mortgage, to buy groceries, to put gas in your car? Once you know, then you're forced to be entrepreneurial because you have a bottom line," she says. I think a lot of people who start businesses, especially services like mine, maybe they don't really *need* to work or they're retired and this is something they want to do on the side. They just kind of go around and they'll try different things and they might not be sure if they're successful or not. I think when you determine how much money you want to make and how you will define success, then you find out if you've got the chops. Can you really make this happen? Can you go out and hustle, hustle, hustle?"

Resilience and determination were key to Tracie O'Keefe, author of the Amazon number one bestseller *Inspiration for Survive and Prosper: Personal Transformation Out of Crisis*, a self-help book on how to quickly recover from trauma or crisis.

"As a child, no one expected me to be successful," she says. "Despite little formal education when I was young, I trained and qualified in over a dozen professions, read at least two hours every single day of my life, educated myself in everything I could. I found the best teachers there were and stuck to them like glue. I defied all the odds to survive and then prosper. I learned that you create yourself in this life according to your own wants, needs, and desires. Set yourself lofty goals and don't give up until you achieve them."

All that said, this doesn't mean you have to stick at something when your heart truly isn't in it. Life is a journey and a process of figuring out your purpose and sometimes the best move is to walk away.

Manage Your Expectations

Being a business owner can seem glamorous, but it's important to be realistic about what it entails.

According to acupuncturist Heather Lounsbury, only five percent of people who train to be acupuncturists stick with it, due to the long hours required to build a business and all the additional aspects outside of the key service.

Tim Barford of Yaoh and VegFestUK warns that while starting a new business can be exciting, maintaining it is the challenge.

"If you're considering running a vegan business, consider first whether you really love it enough to be around 10 years later because, if not, the novelty wears off. Unfortunately, for a lot of us, business becomes that monotony of answering emails, packing orders, sorting out problems for people, dealing with complaints and missing parcels, late deliveries, and the endless general mundane run-of-the mill stuff," says Barford.

Learning how to love the not-so-lovable tasks until you can delegate them is how Linda Doby of Wellinhand, a topical herbal remedies company in Virginia, turned her business from work to play. "I don't feel like I go to work. I never feel like I go to work. I always feel like I'm going out to play and I just happen to be very productive when I'm there," says Doby.

Flexibility and Adaptability

Being able to step aside and get a perspective on where your business is going is essential to staying the course and growing, says Barford. "If you're to survive, you can't stand still. You've got to respond to market changes, different influences, and other people's attitudes, or competitors who will perhaps go down your route, maybe stepping on your toes. You've got to stay one step ahead."

Jessica Bailey agrees. "You can't get set in your ways at all; you have to be very flexible, and you have to let go of stuff as well," she says. "I've been learning about 'owner's syndrome' with businesses where the owners get so embedded and entrenched that they won't let go of things, and that actually impedes the growth of the business. So, no matter how challenging it is, you have to be able to step back and hand over tasks."

Marketer Stephanie Redcross from Vegan Mainstream in Georgia encourages business owners and entrepreneurs to get out of their comfort zones to grow themselves and their businesses.

"We have to develop ourselves as entrepreneurs because, in the past, many of us have worked nine to five, and this is a very different job. Becoming an entrepreneur doesn't automatically mean you have all the skills and experience you need; in fact, there almost certainly will be gaps. So you have to start networking, hanging out with other entrepreneurs, and always be looking to expand your skill set to fill those gaps," says Redcross.

Wally Fry goes further, arguing that laziness and excuses aren't an option when running your own business. "People too often use the excuse of, 'I am not good at this or that sort of stuff.' If you want success, you'd better learn how to be good at a number of things that you feel challenged by or don't particularly like doing. The amazing thing is, most people are capable of most things but need to stretch themselves in the faith that they'll conquer the unknown. Learn and get to grips with the science and nitty gritty of every facet of your business, in the greatest of details, and you will succeed," says Fry.

This is a lesson that Giacomo Marchese, co-founder of Vegan Proteins, a supplement business in Massachusetts, learned. "You have to trust yourself to make decisions and not be attached to the outcome and not fear it. Everything you put in, you get out, and, as much as you want things to happen a certain way, it's still very unpredictable how the outcome of the investment of your time, your energy, and your resources will play out. And you have to roll with those punches," says Marchese.

Veggie Grill's T.K. Pillan likens starting and growing a business to sports. "It's constantly changing because as your business goes through different stages, you have to start developing different skill sets. So it's almost like, in the early stages, you're the personality, you're the all-star player. You jump around making the shots, and, as you grow to different stages, you become more of a coach and even more of a manager and owner. So you have to be ready for the different stages and be able to go through them," says Pillan.

Respond, Rather Than React
As vegans we're exposed on a regular basis to the atrocities of

animal abuse, which is distressing and brings up emotions such as sadness, grief, despair, or anger. If we don't have the tools or techniques to be able to manage ourselves, there's a temptation to react harshly to others, whether in person or online. As noted earlier, this can damage your reputation.

Sometimes, we blame others for making us feel a certain way. I know I did for years, until I saw the quote attributed to Eleanor Roosevelt on social media that said, "No one can make you feel inferior without your permission." It was certainly an eye-opener and puts responsibility on us to choose how we respond in difficult circumstances.

One of the interviewees for this book recounted a story that demonstrates how the energy we send out in challenging situations can influence the outcome. The person asked not to be named in this instance due to the sensitive nature of the situation.

"Our mission statement is, 'We are here to bring connection, creation, inspiration, and beauty to the world,' and that's how I operate in my life and in my shop. We had a theft that happened recently. I could've closed my shop at that point and been very upset and discouraged by this, but, instead, I took it step by step. I watched the video and saw the guy steal, and I educated myself on where I needed to fill the loopholes and education of my staff. I looked to myself and asked, 'What do I need to do to train myself and the people who work for me better?' And I really took it on; this is going to sound completely crazy, but there was a euphoria that I felt after seeing the video. I was very upset, of course, when it happened and very angry at myself and at the staff member who didn't make the best move, but, ultimately, what I'd taken away from it is, 'What do I need to learn?' I just trusted. I trusted that if I stay on track and do what I do, there's a reason why I'm doing this, and it's, of course, something higher than just selling products. And while we were watching the video of the guy stealing, I had another customer call me, and the sale we made covered the loss, so it all fed back to itself."

Take Care of Yourself

In order to be able to respond in a calm and positive way to people and situations, you don't want to be in a state of perpetual stress and burnout. Even though it takes a huge amount of time and energy to start and run a business, it's important not to sacrifice your health—physical, mental, emotional, or spiritual. To be able to thrive, we need enough rest, family time, personal time, creative time, and fun time.

Even as I write this, I'm reminding myself of this—and to not feel guilty for taking time out to relax. Self-care is not self-indulgent. It's as important as every other aspect of running a business.

The vegan business owners interviewed for this book each had their own way of relaxing and recharging. Many practiced yoga, meditation, self-hypnosis, spirituality, and had designated regular family time, time to create, or time to take a walk in nature. Wellinhand's Linda Doby studied for a law degree, while Eva Fung, owner of Canadian handbag, wallet and accessories brand ESPE, enjoyed learning French and how to play the violin.

"One of the challenges that we currently face is not burning out," says Dani Taylor, co-owner of Vegan Proteins. "When you work for yourself, especially if you have a home-based business, you never really get to 'punch out.' Part of this is to be expected and is necessary in getting a business off the ground, but it can become excessive to the point when you're no longer seeing family or friends or making time for anything not work-related.

"When this happens, you actually start to see diminishing returns in your business. You don't realize it sometimes until it's already happening, but scheduling some down time, even if that just means a designated 'unplug' time of day when you're not answering work emails or returning phone calls, can really help keep you motivated, interested, and passionate about your work," says Taylor.

The Regal Vegan's Ella Nemcova stresses the importance of

saying "no" to avoid burnout. "I definitely have to practice self-care," she says. "I think there were a lot of times when I was working around the clock and exhausting myself and not having any fun. There's no doubt about it, starting a business requires a lot of 'no' and that's learning to say 'no' to anything that's not in line with your vision," says Nemcova.

As a naturopath and hypnotherapist, Dr Tracie O'Keefe reminds us to eat a balanced, healthy diet and to exercise at least twice a week, even if it's just walking, because exercise is not only good for our health but for our business too. "I teach people to be the very best they can be, physically and mentally. If you really want to be successful in your business, balance those two elements of your life so you become a high-level performer in your business," says O'Keefe.

Avoid Perfection—Just Do It!

Many business owners "sweat the small stuff" rather than "diving in," says Jessica Burman of Cocoon Apothecary, a concept psychologist Clare Mann agrees with. "It's important to focus on selling your product or service as soon as possible, rather than waiting for it to be perfect. Many people 'prepare to be prepared' and delay selling until they're 150 percent ready, and, without income, they run into trouble," says Mann. "It's important to prioritize your tasks. Many people try to beautify their website or put in place the perfect accounting system. It's best to engage in what I call 'sloppy success' in those areas. You can always, and should, return to these systems and perfect them later when you have the machinery in place to sell. Avoid trying to be perfect. There is always something you could improve on, but if you wait, you could miss the boat."

Confidence Mindset

While humility is a positive trait, insecurity and lack of confidence will hold you back. "I didn't know how to run a business at all, and, in my formal education, they didn't really give any clues on how to do that, so I made my fair share of mistakes," says acupuncturist Heather Lounsbury. "At the beginning, I was desperate to bring in patients and income, and I think people sensed my desperation. I was insecure about building the business, not owning that I'm good at what I do, and I gave away a lot of free sessions to people who didn't really appreciate the work and never came back."

When you're confident in your service or product, you make others confident in it. When a buyer at an upmarket grocery chain in Sydney, Australia, knocked back Bounty Burgers's founder Loren Lembke's request to supply their shops, she refused to take 'no' for an answer.

"I sent the buyer an email and he responded saying they already had fresh vegetarian patties. I persevered nevertheless. Then a few weeks later, his assistant contacted me with his personal phone number, and that's when the phrase came to me, 'When does no mean no?' So I called him and said, 'I can meet you at the store with samples.' That was on a Friday; by the following Monday the 'no' was a 'yes,'" Lembke recalls.

Overwhelm and Time Management
One of the keys to avoid becoming overwhelmed is managing your time and *not* having an "open calendar," advises Stephanie Redcross of Vegan Mainstream.

"When I say 'time management,' I don't mean that in the general way. I mean really having a good idea of what you spend your time on in a day. I tell people to manage their day and manage it on a calendar. For example, if you're going to do social media, put it on your calendar for 30 minutes or an hour, and it doesn't have to be every day.

"Maybe in the beginning, it's Monday, Wednesday, and Friday, and that way, you can get a handle on it. Instead of having '50 tasks I have to do every day,' divide those out over the week and say, 'I'm going to do social media this day, or I'm just going to do Facebook that day.' Get really specific and allocate that time. If you need a block of time in the day for fire drills, issues, customer complaints, talking with employees, and so on, create a time for those things on your calendar as well.

"I believe we often think as business owners that we should have an open calendar for whatever comes our way, and *that's* what does us in. Without a time-sensitive schedule in place, it's easy for a day to run away, and it's also easy to miscalculate how much time you're dedicating to something," says Redcross.

Nichole Dandrea, owner of Nicobella organic chocolates in Georgia, agrees and suggests getting away from the business, even for a short time. "Realize that not everything is going to get done in the day, so take a step back. Take even a 30-minute walk with your dog in the park, and just reset everything. Taking a break from my business to network with others and talk to other small business owners about their experiences has also been really helpful for me," says Dandrea.

Breaking Old Habits and the Six Human Needs

We've only touched briefly on mindset because it's a huge topic, and there are plenty of books dedicated to various aspects of self-growth, including Anthony Robbins's *Awaken the Giant Within* and Ron Prasad's *Welcome to Your Life,* which I recommend and there are others listed in the Resources section.

One of the fastest ways to break old habits and patterns is through hypnosis, and you can check out the downloadable hypnosis programs by my partner, Dr Tracie O'Keefe, an experienced hypnotherapist, naturopath, and business mindset coach, at **www.doctorok.com**.

I'd like to share one model with you before we move on to the next chapter, and that is the Six Human Needs, which was developed by Anthony Robbins. I find it a powerful tool for understanding the drivers behind much of our behavior.

According to Robbins, regardless of what culture or country we're from, whatever our background, we all have six needs that we must fulfill. There's no choice—it's like breathing. We can't wake up one day and decide, "Oh, I don't think I'll bother breathing today." We have to do it.

In the same way, we have to fulfill these six needs. We can either fulfill them in ways that are positive and beneficial to us and our well-being, or we can fulfill them in ways that are detrimental to us. A lot of the time, we're fulfilling these needs unconsciously (in the same way that we're unaware of how certain beliefs impact our lives, which we looked at earlier in this chapter). In other words, we don't realize what we're doing.

Now this is fine if we're meeting the six needs in ways that are good for us and helping us to achieve our goals and dreams. But when we're meeting them in ways that result in us self-sabotaging or doing things that are harmful to us or holding us back or hurting others, then we have to become aware of why we're doing them because only by becoming aware of a problem can you begin to solve it.

So what are the six human needs?

They are:

1. Certainty
2. Variety
3. Significance
4. Love/connection
5. Growth
6. Contribution

The first four are the needs of the ego or personality, the "me" that shows up with all its emotions, dramas and issues.

The final two (growth and contribution) are the needs of what some people call the "higher self," the "soul," the "spirit," "universal consciousness," or even the "God self." Pick whatever word works for you.

The majority of people are driven by certainty—stability, security, and comfort. We like to be in control of ourselves and our environment. We can meet this need unresourcefully by controlling others or watching the same soap opera every night. Or we can meet it resourcefully, such as backing ourselves in our endeavors, or having rituals in our lives that are good for us, such as a fresh fruit smoothie for breakfast each morning.

We all have a need for variety, which is the opposite of certainty. Variety is about risk-taking, adventure, uncertainty, excitement. Again, we can meet our need for variety in ways that are detrimental to us, such as cheating on our partner, causing drama, or sitting in front of the TV and channel hopping. We can meet this need resourcefully by taking up a hobby, meeting new people, eating different foods (vegan of course!).

Our need for significance, to feel special, is often met unresourcefully. We see it played out when someone is desperate for attention and makes everything about *them*. Doing drama (which also meets our need for variety) and putting others down are other, unresourceful ways of meeting our need for significance. To meet this need resourcefully, we can be a *giver* of significance, by praising others, instead of a *getter* of significance. The beauty of this is that the more we do our work in the world and help others, the more we get recognition and significance.

We can ensure we meet our need for love—or connection—by being clingy, staying in unhealthy relationships, or through shared problems. Or we can meet it through healthy, nurturing relationships, or a shared passion or cause.

In regards to the final two needs—growth and contribution—we each desire to grow personally, intellectually, emotionally, and spiritually, as well as do good in the world. When we engage resourcefully with these needs, we tend to meet the previous four needs in a positive and rewarding way.

Out of the six needs, we have what's called a core driver—the need that we must meet at all costs, above any other.

Now that you're aware of this model, it's worth spending some time to discover what your core driver is and the different ways you meet it (both unresourcefully and resourcefully).

There's a lot more to the Six Human Needs model than there's room for in this book, including how it can be used to disrupt procrastination and what it means for your relationships, both personal and professional. When you know what another person's core driver is, you can communicate with them much better.

If you'd like to know more about this model so you can use it to grow yourself and your business, you can purchase an ebook and audio program I put together. Go to **www.veganbusinessmedia. com/six-human-needs** to download it.

Chapter 3
Set-Up, Structure, Systems

So, you're clear on your purpose, have started your personal growth journey, and decided you want to run your own business. Where do you begin?

There's a lot to consider before starting your operation. These are some of the questions you need to get clear on:

- Will you run your business from a physical premises, be home-based, or be online?
- Will you service a local, national, or international market?
- Will you set up as a sole trader/proprietorship, partnership, limited company, or corporation?
- What, if any, staff will you take on immediately?
- What equipment do you need?
- What systems and tools do you need in place to operate your business?
- Which of these are essential to have right now?
- Do you want to build a business to sell in the future?
- Do you want to build your business around you as a thought leader?
- How will you fund your business to begin with and into the future?
- How big and/or fast do you want to grow?
- Will you start a new business from scratch, buy an existing business, or take on a franchise?

Some of your answers to the above will come back to your "why." What kind of lifestyle do you want? How much work/life balance is agreeable to you?

"When I started, I wasn't sure if I was going to go into a product business, open a restaurant, run a delivery business, or if I was going to have a wellness center," admits The Regal Vegan's Ella Nemcova. "I had so many ideas of what I wanted to do, and the only way I was able to fine tune my business direction was to talk to a lot of people so I could get clear. Is your freedom at all important to you? You need to decide what kind of life you want to live."

Honesty is essential here. Meditate on what you truly desire from your life and business, and don't just decide on what other people think you should have, or what *you* think you *should* have. It's your dream. It's important to be true to yourself and the type of business you truly desire to run.

"If I've heard it once, I've heard it a hundred times: Why don't you put the academy online?" says author Victoria Moran, founder of vegan lifestyle coaching program Main Street Vegan Academy. "They tell me, 'So many more people could do it if it was online, and you could make so much more money, and blah blah.' But that's not the point, and what I tell them is that if they want to go to Harvard, they travel to Massachusetts; if they want to go to Oxford, they travel to England; and if they want to go to Main Street Vegan Academy, they travel to New York City for six days. And I understand that it's difficult and there's expense involved and they have to find a place to stay, and if they've never been to New York, it seems big and scary, but that's part of the experience. So when you get your idea for what you want to do in the world, listen for that inspiration that comes from within you," says Moran.

The Importance of Market Research

Before you set up any business, you must do your market research to make sure you have a viable product or service. While the aim is to do what you love, it also has to pay the bills and give you the lifestyle you want; otherwise, it's a hobby, not a business.

Creating a product or a service because you think your market will rush to buy it isn't the way to go. You'll have spent considerable time and money putting it together, but if no one's buying it, you'll have wasted both.

"If you're somebody who wants to start a bakery, and you see that, just as a home cook, no matter how fancy you got with your baking, everybody really wanted your basic chocolate chip cookies, well that tells you something," says Moran. "You can do all the fancy stuff in your bakery, but those chocolate chip cookies are what people really want. I think so often people have a business idea because they think that's what they *should* do, but that's not it. You have to have a business idea for a product or service that people want."

You don't necessarily have to hire an expensive market research firm, but you do need to hang out where your target market is, talk to them, tell them what you're planning, and gauge the interest. How much competition is there? Competition isn't a bad thing, as it shows there's demand for that product or service. Your job is to come up with a point of difference that shows why you're better than the others.

Eco-Vegan Gal's Whitney Lauritsen says the key mistake new business owners make is assuming they know what their market wants. "They don't do their research, especially when it comes to market testing and understanding what their audience wants. What they want to do may not be reflective of what the market needs or wants, which can result in failure," says Lauritsen.

Just because you're planning to start a business run on vegan principles doesn't automatically guarantee success, despite the vegan community being loyal consumers.

Finance expert Lee Coates, director of Ethical Investors in the UK and Cruelty Free Super in Australia, agrees. "It's great that you're ethical, but you have to do your research. You need to look at what business area you're going to be in and then you say, 'How can I do that business ethically?' Not, 'I'm going to be ethical and I'm going to do something that nobody wants.' That perpetuates the myth that if you're ethical, you don't succeed or, 'There's another failed ethical business.'

"It failed because nobody wanted the product. Whether it was ethical or exploitative, it still would have failed. So you have to say, 'This is a service people want. I can do this and I believe I'm really good at it; now how can I do it ethically and responsibly?' And if you do it in that order, then the business will succeed because people will see that it's driven by values but it's also something that they want," says Coates.

Once you've conducted your research and found there's a market for your product or service, you then have to figure out what Tofurky's Seth Tibbott calls your "unfair advantage." "It's a leap of faith to start a business. Knowing what your skill set is and what your unfair advantage is that you have over all the other businesses that are maybe starting out in this area is important," says Tibbott.

"In the beginning, my unfair advantage was that I had already made tempeh for years in my home, so I knew a bit more. There were all these little tempeh shops starting up but they didn't know as much as me.

"With Tofurky, our unfair advantage was we were the first ones to the market with it. There were other brands that soon came on and tried to duplicate it, but because the story was new for us, we had all this press and brand awareness, and that really created an unfair advantage for us. Maybe your unfair advantage is you're a wizard at marketing, you have a friend at an advertising firm who's willing to work for cheap to get the word out, or you have access to a celebrity who may endorse your offering," says Tibbott.

Samantha Crosby, founder of skincare line Ayana Organics in Australia, is a good example of a business owner identifying a gap in a market and claiming her unfair advantage. "I saw a gap in the market for vegans with vegan babies. Most natural products for pregnant women in Perth, Western Australia, contained animal products or by-products. Many contained potentially toxic ingredients. I saw a gap in the market, and went about filling it, in keeping with my ethics. I'd advise not to create a product or service until you've established a clear need for it," says Crosby.

Have a Business Plan

If, like me, you're resistant to the phrase *Business Plan* because of its droll-sounding name, call it something else, such as Vision Map or Vegan World Domination Scheme. But you need one. It doesn't have to be overly complex. Some business plan templates are daunting with their endless pages, so if you feel overwhelmed, use a simplified version.

You may think you have everything about your business idea all sorted in your head, but committing it to paper (or computer file) gets it out, and you can see clearly any shortcomings. And as you write or type, you'll likely get on a creative roll and come up with fabulous new ideas and aspects you hadn't considered before.

A business plan is a document that maps out your goals for the business along with details of how you plan to achieve them. It considers aspects such as what your business is, its aims, who your target market is, how you'll reach them, how you'll fund the business at start up and further in, what your unique selling proposition (point of difference) is, cost and sales projections, strategies for growth, and more.

A business plan is useful not only for you as the owner to focus your strategies and track milestones but also, if you're seeking investors, they'll expect to see a formal business plan. The same is true if you're applying for a commercial loan.

"A lot of people come to me and ask me about starting a business doing this and that and many of them are quite far down the line with it. I ask them if they have a business plan, and they say, 'What?'" says Tim Barford of Yaoh and VegFestUK.

"You've got to make sure that your passion and enthusiasm for a project, which obviously you're going to need to start any business, doesn't completely exclude attention to margins, overheads, legalities, competition, some kind of idea how you're going to market your products, how you're going to sell them, how stable your production is. There's quite a lot of key issues to look into, and a business plan helps to uncover and track them."

How Big and/or Fast Do You Want to Grow?

There's a temptation, when starting a business, to grow as quickly as possible. It's understandable as friends and family may have put you off the idea, worried that you'll fail and have no security without a 'proper job.' You want to put their minds at ease and prove that you can do this, so you start to grow too fast. You may even be tempted to appear bigger than you actually are.

There are several pitfalls to this approach. "Oftentimes, when an entrepreneur starts a new business, they make the mistake of assuming that they're like a corporate business they admire, or supposing they're similar to XYZ business," says Vegan Mainstream's Stephanie Redcross. "But a business that's in year one is very different than a business that's in year 10. So, while it's good to have aspirations and goals, it's very difficult to act on them immediately, unless you have a ton of capital and a boatload of money coming in. It's foolhardy to operate a business as a solo entrepreneur the same way you would operate a business that has 50 employees. It's important to make sure you understand the difference between your aspirations and what you're capable of doing and achieving *now*."

For example, Redcross warns against spending hundreds of dollars getting your first videos edited or printing up 10,000 copies of a flashy business card. "I'm not saying don't get business cards, or make them look bad. But you don't want to have thousands of fancy, expensive cards sitting in your closet because, a year or two from now, a lot of that stuff will have changed."

Trying to act bigger than they are is one reason why some small businesses fail, says Redcross. "If you're a small business, operate like a small business until you're a medium-sized business. Because if you don't, that's when it's easy to get into financial trouble. When people start trying to look bigger than they are, they start getting into lines of credit and so forth, and things can quickly go sideways. So play it safe as you're getting started and run your business without running a debt."

Focus on how to get your first few customers, says Redcross. "Don't think, 'How do I get 10,000 customers?' First, get 20 customers if you've had no customers before. Because once you get 20 customers you can figure out how to get 40, and then how to get 200, and so on. Operate in your lane, and do that exceptionally well before moving up to the next level."

Comparison is the thief of joy, according to a quote attributed to Theodore Roosevelt, and, as Redcross notes, you have the potential to damage your business, as well as your self-esteem, by comparing yourself to larger brands. Far better to take a leaf out of Vegan Proteins's co-owner Giacomo Marchese's playbook and embrace where you are right now.

"Obviously, we're not an Amazon; we can't compete with them," he says. "We thought about doing our shipping out of a fulfillment center instead of from our home office, and maybe it would've helped us more, but we found we really love the customer service; we love how it impacts other people. It's a little harder and not as cost-effective, but we're not trying to be some giant business. We're not working on a corporate business model. We're happy with being a small-sized business and maybe one day being a mid-sized business," says Marchese.

It comes back to your goals for your business and lifestyle—your "why." Nichole Dandrea is clear that she doesn't want Nicobella to be a multimillion-dollar chocolate business; instead, she wants a lifestyle business that's sustainable and allows her to spend time with family.

Los Angeles-based vegan actor and jewelry designer Ele Keats also doesn't want an "out of control" jewelry brand. "I personally want to live and enjoy my life and enjoy all my other activities. I don't want my business to consume me to a level where I'm not able to take a vacation and enjoy my friends and my family and my beloveds. It's a different business model. Some people want to be so successful that everybody knows their name; that's not where I'm at. Quality of life is the most important thing to me," says Keats.

Tofurky's Seth Tibbott is also wary of businesses growing too fast. "We grew very differently than most of the start-ups I see today. Some of them, from day one, are paying themselves some pretty big salaries. They're not even selling yet, and they're paying these big salaries. And there's quite a few companies here in the US that have now gone to Silicon Valley and gotten big investments from outside investors, so before they even make any money at all, they're in debt up to their eyeballs," says Tibbott.

Running your own business is a steep learning curve and you will make mistakes, so it's better to make small screw-ups than huge ones. Starting out on a market stall like Vx shop owner Rudy Penando did in London's Camden Markets is a smart way to test the market and build up a loyal clientele instead of rushing headfirst into opening a physical shop with massive overheads.

Tim Barford of Yaoh hemp products cites the example of several of his competitors growing too quickly and then getting into trouble when the Global Financial Crisis (GFC) of 2008 hit. "They invested in new premises, new equipment, new branding, and staff. They may have gone from a team of four or five to a team of 12 or 15, with a little office and IT equipment and everything to match. But their projected profits didn't happen, which caused a lot of problems for them. In the case of Yaoh, we didn't grow that much; we held tight and just about managed to stay in business," says Barford.

On the other hand, Tracy Perkins's Strawberry Hedgehog

skincare business in Arizona saw its initial success during the GFC. Since then, she's grown the business slowly and steadily. "I lost my teaching job with the initial downturn and needed to boost the income from my business," she explains. "I started selling at farmers' markets, doing more 'hands-on' work as opposed to 100 percent online sales. I reached out to large local retailers and won a wholesale account with Whole Foods in Arizona in 2009. I've been very patient with my business, allowing it to grow slowly over the years. It's only recently that it's been possible to pay my bills with the income, but it's that slow growth that has allowed it to be sustained," says Perkins.

If you've grown your business too fast, it's okay to scale back. This doesn't equal failure. "Maybe you expanded too fast, or tried to do too much. You went into 10 farmers' markets and it's driving you crazy, you're exhausted, maybe the quality of your food is starting to suffer, and so forth. Cut back," says Stephanie Redcross. "There's nothing wrong with cutting back, and I think sometimes our pride gets in the way. We're concerned that it won't look good. But you're a business owner now and you have to make smart, big decisions. In this day and age, you can tell your customers what you're doing. You can say you're cutting back and tell them why.

"Sometimes people get so nervous that they run and hide. We tell ourselves, 'Oh I couldn't do that, I'm such a failure!' But you're not a failure. This is you making a responsible business assessment and doing what makes sense at this time. Cutting back now, and going bigger again six months or a year from now, is much smarter than potentially bleeding your business dry because you've expanded too quickly and allowed shame and fear to keep you from making good decisions," says Redcross.

Sugandh G. Agrawal from GUNAS can relate to this. She recognized that she was doing too much too quickly by putting out four to five handbag collections each year, so she scaled it back to two or maximum three a year, allowing her the time to strategize to grow the business at a pace that matched the lifestyle she wanted.

"I see, a lot of times, people start burning out, putting in long hours each week because they want to get successful really quickly. I understand that the vegan market is a niche one and people want to capture it before a lot of players have gotten to it. But I feel it's such a new market that we still have time, and we still have plenty of stores to sell our bags to, plenty of other brands that could even still come in and make a difference. I take one day at a time, and, because I'm going at a steady and maybe a much slower pace, as compared to other brands, I feel like this is helping me to learn a lot more and rectify the mistakes that I might be making with my company or with my brand and really understand my target audience," says Agrawal.

That said, not everyone who starts out big fails. The founders of Veggie Grill knew from the beginning that they wanted a chain, rather than one or two restaurants. "This was our vision. Not having been in the restaurant business before, we weren't here just to start a café and be in the restaurant business. We were doing it because we thought there was an opportunity to make a big difference in our country and the world, and the way to do that is by creating a chain, not just one or two," says T.K. Pillan.

Victoria Moran believes it can sometimes be advantageous for smaller businesses to think like big conglomerates from the start, particularly to enable different income streams. For example, Moran created Main Street Vegan Enterprises as an umbrella operation that houses Main Street Vegan Academy, which trains vegan lifestyle coaches. Another arm of the business is Main Street Productions which is currently producing a film, *Miss Liberty*, about a cow who escapes from a slaughterhouse; then there's the *Main Street Vegan* book, blog, and podcasts, plus Moran's other books with a vegan message.

Do You Want to Work on *or* in *Your Business?*

According to Michael Gerber, author of the renowned book *The E-Myth* (Entrepreneurial Myth), most new businesses are started by what he calls "technicians", who love the hands-on aspect of the work, rather than entrepreneurs, who set out to create, grow, and lead a solid business.

A technician works *in* the business, while an entrepreneur works *on* the business—that is, strategizing, looking at the big picture, brainstorming ideas for improvement or expansion.

The third personality identified by Gerber is the "manager." Unlike the entrepreneur, who is an innovator and creative thinker, the manager is pragmatic—a planner and organizer.

When these three come together—either with different people in larger companies or as aspects of one person in the case of a solo operator—a business stands the best chance of succeeding, rather than if it's built by a technician alone.

The realities of running a business are often a shock to new business owners, especially those who've been used to working as an employee, with regular hours and paycheck, sick leave, health insurance, and paid holidays.

"The field I'm in is full of very creative people who want to help others look and feel great," says image consultant Ginger Burr. "That's wonderful, but unless you have the business skills, or can hire someone who does, you won't survive. You spend part of your time working with your clients, but you also have to do the marketing, administrative tasks, bookkeeping, record keeping, and so on, and, often, in the beginning, you have to do all of those things yourself."

Renia Pruchnicki, owner of the Canadian belt company Truth Belts, found as her business developed, she was forced to move out of the technician role and more into the entrepreneur role. "In the earlier years, I was working in the business and doing everything, including sewing everything, whereas now I can't do that anymore. I very rarely sew. I spend most of my days looking at my computer screen and analyzing charts and spreadsheets," says Pruchnicki.

Mellissa Morgan, founder of Ms. Cupcake, a vegan bakery in the UK's South London, came to the same conclusion early on in her business. "I started Ms. Cupcake as a home business where I was baking the cakes, selling the cakes, doing the administration, and, within a few months, I realized that, as a business owner, I had to ask myself the question: 'Do you want to make cakes for a living? Or do you want to run a cake business?' And this can be transferrable to so many different industries. If you want to make vegan cakes for your living, then go get a job somewhere else where you can get paid to make vegan cakes and save yourself the hassle of running your own business," says Morgan.

If the answer to the question is you want to run a business, then you must accept the fact that you need to hire people quite early to help out. Figure out what you're best at and love doing; then do that and bring on staff to do the rest. "For some people, it might be social media; for others, it might be the accounts. For me, it was that I didn't like making butter cream icing, so I got someone to fill that role in my business; and that's how the business grew step by step," says Morgan, who realized she had to step back from her business to enable it to grow.

"I had a turning point about two years ago when I realized that we were just treading water, and it was because I wasn't stepping back enough, and now, a huge part of what I do is stepping away from the business and looking not just at the grand picture of growth but also at how we can become more efficient and be an even better place to work for my team."

Manufacturer or Marketer?

For those of you considering starting a product-based business, a key consideration is whether to be a manufacturer or to become a brand and marketing company.

These are two distinct routes to go down, according to

Adrian Ling, managing director of Plamil Foods, which has manufacturing at the heart of its operations, even manufacturing competitors' products. "There are virtually no other brands that produce all-vegan foods themselves in the UK; a lot of companies buy the end product and remold or remake it," says Ling. "For instance, in chocolate, we are a core manufacturer, which means we supply the chocolate that other companies will use to manufacture their own brands. So, we will compete on shelf with a different brand where we are actually the primary manufacturer, and the same with many other different products."

Getting your products into a retail outlet can be challenging. It comes back to knowing you have enough of a market that will buy your product in a particular geographical area. In this scenario, you're not just marketing to the consumer, you also have to market to those who will decide whether to carry those lines wholesale or retail.

"You can have a great product that you think consumers will love, but if retailers don't think they're going to sell enough of those units or more of them than a similar product, it's very difficult for them to justify stocking your product, and, therefore, you have zero sales," says Ling.

Money, Money, Money!

Depending on your perspective, money may or may not, as the character of Sally Bowles in *Cabaret* says, "make the world go round," but it certainly will determine the success or otherwise of your business.

As we saw in the previous chapter on mindset, harboring negative attitudes toward money will sabotage your business. You need to attract it to you, rather than repel it.

The majority of businesses, even online-only ones, will require some kind of start-up capital. How you raise this will depend on a number of factors, including your money rules (what you're willing to do or not do in regards to finance) and the amount of control you want over your business.

Lee Coates urges new business owners to use their own savings if they can and advises against approaching banks for loans in the beginning. "Going into your own business is like jumping off a cliff but you can jump with or without a parachute. It's generally advisable to have a parachute in place," says Coates.

With his first venture, financial management firm Ethical Investors, Coates used his own savings to cover his living costs until the business was able to pay him. With Cruelty Free Super (an Australian superannuation fund), there were high set-up costs, so he found investors who were interested in the idea.

"The last option I would go for would be a bank loan," he asserts. "You need to get to a position where you can show them you've been successful for a bank to then loan you money to continue to grow. They will rarely give it to you in the beginning, unless you sign over your house or similar collateral. If you have a unique and innovative idea, a bank will probably deny you a loan because unique and innovative sounds a bit too risky, and, most of the time, bank staff don't know anything about running a business," says Coates.

Hypnotherapist, naturopath, and business mindset coach Dr Tracie O'Keefe, who has run many businesses since the age of 15, also advises people to start up with their own money. "My first business was funded by me working three part-time jobs while also going to college. The greatest motivator is to put your own money into starting your business. When you lose your own money, that soon wakes you up. Prove you can create turnover before you seek loans or investors," says O'Keefe.

If you must borrow money, pay it back "pronto," says Wally Fry, founder of Fry's Family Foods. "Then you won't work for a bank but for yourself. If you can't buy it with positive money balances, then you don't need it. Because of this philosophy, I'm never over a barrel come decision time. I always know that I can shut up shop, if need be, and the banks aren't going to be taking the shirt off my back. I'm free to enjoy the product of my work. I think this is the one thing that I learned and applied, and it made us different from other businesses out there. Having said that, this sometimes means you have to work a little bit harder without all the 'nice to haves' in your business. The progress might be slow and steady, rather than fast and precarious," says Fry.

Don't be afraid to get a job while you're starting or growing your business—whether part time or even full time. Many businesses aren't profitable until after the first couple of years, so if you don't have savings, having regular income through a job will take the financial pressure off and allow you to cover your living and some business costs.

Truth Belts's Renia Pruchnicki started her business with a small loan plus savings and then had to get a job. "I realized after a year of running my business that I wasn't making any money to support myself, so I got a full-time job and ran my company in the evenings and weekends. Eventually, the full-time job turned into a part-time one. I now run Truth Belts full time."

Mellissa Morgan also recommends finding additional work or going part time in your current position if you can. "I phased out my teaching career while I was investing in starting Ms. Cupcake because you're learning how to run a business, you're making mistakes, you're learning from those mistakes, and if you're worried about how you're going to pay your rent on top of all of that, you're not going to be thinking logically about the business," says Morgan.

Having this outside income, whether through savings or a job, prevents you from being "desperate" to sell your products or services in your burgeoning business, says Ginger Burr. "If you don't have money to support yourself while you're building your business, you will eventually be operating your business out of desperation, and that gets old and not fun very fast."

One of the mistakes new business owners make is underestimating costs—of production, materials, set-up, equipment, insurance, legalities, and so on—which is another good reason to start small and grow slowly. "Don't carry a lot of stock, until you know what your demand is," says Olsenhaus's Elizabeth Olsen.

Running an ethical business, as well as a smaller business, can mean paying higher costs, especially for ingredients or raw materials since you're buying in smaller quantities that don't qualify you for the bulk discounts granted to larger companies.

This requires you to get creative, as Sugandh G. Agrawal had to do when the production costs for her handbags put their retail price out of range for her market. "To keep your prices down, you need to have small-scale production. Because our market is so niche, there's no way I could use a Chinese factory or a large-scale factory to produce a thousand pieces and then have a bunch that I won't be able to sell. So my real big challenge of keeping the price point down was getting production that was ethical and, at the same time, that would do short runs," Agrawal explains.

Initially, she manufactured in New York but found that potential customers kept questioning the price point of her bags, and she wanted to make them more affordable, without compromising on quality or ethics. "I went to China to look at factories over there and really the conditions are awful," she says. "I would never want to sell a product where the people are disconnected from the behind-the-scenes of how the product is made."

Agrawal's solution was to start her own manufacturing studio in India, keeping her production costs lower by working with local women and artisans who are paid a fair wage and work in a comfortable environment. "That helped push me and the brand in the right direction with ethical manufacturing and vegan materials," she says.

On the subject of pricing your product or services, David Benzaquen from PlantBased Solutions offers the following observations:

"One key consideration is how to use effective market research to determine what would sway non-vegan audiences to purchase or consume your product. In doing this, you can ensure that your branding and messaging appeals and relates to these audiences.

"Another is to be sensitive in pricing your product or service to be accessible. Pricing models are traditionally based on value (what consumers are *willing* to pay for this product or service); competition (what my competitors are charging and how I can position myself against them to differentiate my product or service or to not stray too much from what's considered acceptable); or cost (what it costs me to produce this product).

"While a good pricing model should consider all three components, you must question who you're referring to when you ask what consumers are willing to pay for something. If a product were 10 percent cheaper, would it open up access to a whole other group of consumers who may need it more? Benefit from it more? Impact the world in a larger way by embracing vegan products?" says Benzaquen.

Remember that it can take a while to be profitable. As we saw in the previous chapter, it took Seth Tibbott nearly 20 years to turn the corner. "For the first 15 years before Tofurky, I was just making tempeh, and I was making very little money," he admits. "I was living on $300 a month, and that's when I built a treehouse because I didn't have any money to afford the rent of a real house. I rented three trees for $25 a month and spent $1,000 building this treehouse, which I lived in for eight years while I was getting going."

Nowadays, new business owners have an option to raise money for their venture that was unavailable to their predecessors, and that's crowdfunding. Not only artists, authors, and other creatives but entrepreneurs are also taking advantage of the various platforms that enable supporters of a venture to contribute funds to make it happen.

Rabbit Food Grocery, a vegan store that opened in Austin, Texas in February 2015, successfully raised $15,000 on Kickstarter. Antidote Superalimentation smoothie and juice bar in

Montreal raised $45,000 on Indiegogo. *Laika* magazine in New York raised $25,000 on Kickstarter. Premium Chocolatiers in New Jersey raised $47,000 on Kickstarter to make chocolate candies. Beyond Skin vegan shoe company in the UK raised £21,000 on Kickstarter to expand their business; and Superfood Sushi in Australia raised $9,000 on Pozible.

Setting up and promoting a crowdfunding campaign requires considerable time and effort for it to be successful, so before rushing into it, check out this article, "How to Successfully Crowdfund Your Vegan Business," by Demetrius Bagley on the Vegan Business Media website. Bagley is producer of the award-winning documentary *Vegucated* and a much sought-after business adviser: **www.veganbusinessmedia.com/how-to-successfully-crowdfund-your-vegan-business**

Structure
The considerations mentioned earlier in this chapter, such as lifestyle and business growth, will have a bearing on how you structure your business. There are different types of business entities depending on where you're located, and each has its own advantages and disadvantages. The main ones are:

Sole trader or proprietor
You alone are responsible for the business and its assets and liabilities. It's generally the least expensive to set up, but if things go wrong, your personal assets can be seized. Tax implications vary from country to country.

Partnership
This is where one or more people come together to form a business. There are different types of partnerships, some with limited liability.

Company or corporation
A company is a separate legal entity from an individual. It has

limited liability, greater administrative and reporting duties, and higher set-up costs.

Some businesses start out as a sole proprietorship and later switch to becoming incorporated, while others go straight into an incorporated structure.

As noted above, there are advantages and disadvantages to each structure that are beyond the scope of this book.

Consider all the options available to you in your country and get advice from your local business or government department as to what is best for you. There are links in the resources section at the back of this book for the US, UK, Australia, and Canada.

When hiring professionals to help you with these matters, make sure they're qualified financial planners or tax consultants so you get expert help for your personal situation.

Location

If you plan to run a business in a particular geographical area, you must be sure there are enough people interested in what you have to offer; otherwise, your business won't survive.

While metropolitan cities such as New York or Los Angeles may be able to host a range of vegan eateries, a more suburban or rural area may not attract enough of a clientele to keep you afloat. This is why it's imperative to do your market research.

"You've got to really understand who your clients are, where they congregate, and what will make a successful location on a consistent basis," says Veggie Grill's T.K. Pillan. "For our restaurants, the number of pure veggie eaters within our trade areas wouldn't be enough to support our business. If you're like us, where you're doing a retail business that's based on your location, you have to make sure that you test your product and that it's going to have appeal to those who aren't vegan.

"You have to figure out how you make sure that you consistently deliver on a national level or on a multi-regional level.

And how do you make sure that you can hire and train people properly in different regions? And then how do you make sure that, as you go to other regions, you continue to have a feel for what the right locations are? Having a specialized or a less mainstream target market, I think we have to continue to be selective about our locations," says Pillan.

222 Veggie Vegan's Ben Asamani agrees. "I found it difficult to find the location that I wanted. Location is very important. If the location is wrong, you will find it very difficult to be successful. That's why, sometimes, you find vegetarian restaurants open up and then they close down," he says.

Even the wildly successful phenomenon that is the Candle Cafe enterprise in New York had a worrying few months in its early days when owners Joy Pierson and Bart Potenza moved the location and few customers came.

Are your customers prepared to travel to you? Are you prepared to travel to them? Sometimes, you have to go against the grain of what's considered standard in your industry.

Lee Coates found that working in financial services, from an environmental perspective, and being an ethical company meant the business couldn't operate in a localized area like most financial planners in the UK.

"We had to go national to find those people who wanted to invest ethically. And I didn't want to be traveling across the country every other day, so I said to people, 'We'll offer advice based on your needs, but we'll do it remotely.' That meant I didn't have to pay for any traveling, so my cost base was much lower. Half of our clients over a period of 25 years have never met one of our advisers in person," says Coates.

Lifestyle, as Coates touches on, is also an important consideration not only for you but also for your staff. Seth Tibbott hired a senior executive who took the job at a slightly lower salary because she wanted to work at Tofurky's headquarters in the beautiful surroundings of Hood River in Oregon.

Sometimes, your location will change as your business grows or adapts. Donna Oakes-Jones from Cow Jones Industrials started out with a physical shop in upstate New York, then moved online, while Strawberry Hedgehog's Tracy Perkins and The Cruelty Free Shop's Jessica Bailey expanded their online businesses into physical premises.

Obviously, the latter move involves a substantial increase in overheads, so again, make sure you do your research and have evidence that you have a big enough market to sustain you.

Be Flexible About Your Business Offerings

Often, when you start out in your business, you may have a particular idea of how it will operate. But sometimes, it doesn't end up how you envisage, and you must be prepared to be flexible.

JL Fields, for example, was convinced she was going to make her living solely as a vegan lifestyle coach, after completing Victoria Moran's Main Street Vegan Academy course. "I'd been blogging for about three years and I was sure that as soon as I put I was offering vegan lifestyle coaching on my website, I'd have all these clients," she recalls.

When this didn't eventuate, Fields got creative and made a list of all the skills and knowledge she had accrued from her 25-year professional career fundraising in the non-profit sector.

"I started to find other ways to do what I wanted to do with individuals, so I set up public classes in vegan eating," she explains. "I also started reaching out to companies that might need someone to write some language for them around reaching a plant-based audience. I envisioned my business to be in writing, coaching, and teaching, and I wanted all that to be around veganism. But I also understood it wasn't going to happen overnight, so I got in touch with some companies that were connected to my old career and took small, short-term consulting projects with them so I could make some money while I spent my time building my business up," says Fields.

Now a successful author and freelance writer, Fields also provides corporate trainings where she goes into a company and offers a six-week cooking class with their employees, makes and delivers vegan meals in her local area, and does one-on-one vegan lifestyle coaching.

Fields is an excellent example of someone who has created multiple streams of income. "For my business to work, I need all of those revenue streams because if one closes up, which it will, it doesn't plunge me into a difficult situation," she says.

Changing economic climates also call for flexibility, as Kendall Hayes, owner of two Iku Wholefood franchises in Sydney's central business district, found out. As more firms left the city, chasing cheaper office rents in the suburbs, Hayes added an online shop and delivery service to busy executives and employees who are not able to leave their desks for lunch.

Systems and Tools

Depending on what type of business you run, you'll need various systems and tools. Some may be specific to your industry, such as special software for stock control or particular equipment.

But there are some systems and tools that are necessary for all businesses. A good accounting system is essential. You don't need to invest in an expensive one, and, when starting out, you may even use spreadsheets, but you do need to keep clear and concise records of your income and expenditure. The last thing you want is the government to find fault and fine you. So invest in a system that will help you keep your accounts in order.

A customer relationship management system (CRM) is also key. What these programs do is keep records of your clients and enable you to keep in touch with them, provided they have agreed to receive information from you. Do *not* add someone to your database without their permission. It's much easier (and less expensive) to get existing (happy) customers to buy from you again than to chase new leads. Now, this is not to say you need to rush out and immediately buy an expensive system before you're making money. Fortunately, there are plenty of low-cost CRM services available that are tailored for small businesses, and you can check some of those out in the Resources section on Vegan Business Media: **www.veganbusinessmedia.com/resources**

Once your business grows and you're bringing in income, you can then invest in higher-end systems. This is how New York-based vegan cheese maker Pablo Castro of Dr-Cow did things. "At first you do something in a small batch with probably some home appliances to get the right recipe and the right final product but when you want to scale up, everything changes. Getting the right equipment and machinery is key," says Castro.

On-site and mobile credit card facilities are important, more so than ever now, as fewer people buy goods and services with cash or checks. And if you exhibit at expos, being able to process card transactions instead of forcing potential customers to extract cash from an ATM will help your bottom line tremendously.

If you're the sort of person for whom "systems" and "organization" are anathema, this is your opportunity to grow and get out of your comfort zone! Creatives often find it hard to systematize, preferring to "go with the flow." But if you want your business to run smoothly, you must be organized.

"I'm a writer and artist," says Victoria Moran. "In my writer-only life, I didn't need any systems. I'd just go to a café and plug in. But it's not like that when people are depending on you. With the academy, I have people coming from different parts of the world who have bought expensive plane tickets, so everything needs to run like a well-oiled machine."

Jivamukti Yoga school co-founder Sharon Gannon agrees. Running a hugely successful school in New York, with several studios internationally, requires detailed systems. A renowned author, Gannon jokes that she's spent more time writing procedural manuals than books.

"What I learned above and beyond anything else is the importance of communication; to be very clear when speaking to your employees, your teachers, your students, everybody," she says. "That means writing things down. I've written a lot of yoga books, but most of the writing I've done has been procedural manuals for my staff so there's no guessing on their part. When you write things down and you clearly communicate, you give the person you're speaking to confidence. They don't have to second guess your intention and be in a state of fear, wondering, 'Am I doing my job right?' or, 'Is my boss going to yell at me?' "I don't want that kind of atmosphere of fear among my staff. I want it to be very clear; everything transparent and communicated very well," says Gannon.

Nowadays, there are a multitude of apps and technology designed to improve our lives. Some of it's great, but it's also easy to fall down the rabbit hole of "shiny new thing" and spend too much time searching for something that will supposedly give us back time and make our jobs easier. Make a list of "must-haves" and "nice-to-haves" and focus on the former to begin with.

Chapter 4
Relationships

The success of your business depends on the quality of your relationships, particularly with:
- Yourself
- Your family
- Clients/customers
- Staff
- Consultants and other professionals
- Suppliers, wholesalers, retailers and manufacturers
- Collaborators and competitors
- Adversaries

Relationship with Yourself
We covered much of this in the chapter on mindset, but it's worth repeating to stress the importance of how you manage yourself because this will impact how you manage your relationships with the other stakeholders listed above.

If you're quick to anger and communicate in a way that's perceived as unfriendly, unhelpful, aggressive, or patronizing, people won't want to work with or for you. When you're a business owner, you become a leader. Being an ethical leader requires good self-leadership to begin with.

Learning to communicate effectively with others in a way that warms them to you and your brand is how you get regular customers and referrals.

Relationship with Family
Family is however you define it—romantic or life partner(s),

friends, blood family, legal family, or chosen family.

We covered in Chapter 2 the need to find a balance between running your business and spending quality time with your family. This quality time contributes to your well-being, which, in turn, allows you to run your business more efficiently.

If your business is impacting negatively on your relationship with your family, this needs to be addressed. The costs in running a business aren't just financial. Ask yourself regularly: Is it worth it?

This doesn't mean there won't be times when you have to go full out and sacrifice some leisure and family time, but put a time limit on it, like Ms. Cupcake's Mellissa Morgan did. "When I started this business, I said to my husband and my son, 'You need to give me two years, and if, by then, I don't have a very clear path and goals and be able to work away from the business, I will stop everything,'" says Morgan. "And that gave me a kick up the backside to really dedicate everything in those first two years that I needed to do so that I would have that time in two years to say, 'Okay, where am I? Is this where I want to be?'"

It's important that the time you do spend in your relationships with others is high quality and this is equally true of your relationship with your significant other if you have one. Author Barbara DeAngelis, in *How to Make Love All the Time*, highlights the four phases that can kill a relationship:

Resistance: You feel uncomfortable or dislike something your partner says or does. If resistance is not communicated, it turns into:

Resentment: Your annoyance with your partner turns into anger and you erect an emotional barrier. Resentment destroys intimacy in a relationship and results in:

Rejection: If resentment is not dealt with, it leads to you rejecting your partner by separating emotionally and physically from them. Everything they do and say is wrong. This leads to:

Repression: To protect yourself from the pain of the above, you repress your emotions by becoming numb, losing any passion or excitement that once existed.

To avoid the four Rs, open and honest communication is crucial. Anthony Robbins, in *Awaken the Giant Within,* reminds us that if we want our relationships to last, never threaten to leave the relationship, and take time each day to remind ourselves of our partner's positive attributes and how lucky we are to be with them. (Obviously, this doesn't apply to abusive situations.)

What if you work with your partner in the business? This can present certain challenges, since you're together pretty much 24/7 and the stresses of running a business can rub off onto your relationship. Understanding each other's strengths and weaknesses, along with clear, calm communication can result in a more harmonious business and personal relationship, as Amanda Solomons and Simone Bateman, who run Rubyfruit café in the Blue Mountains, Australia, found.

"I'm naturally a dreadfully unorganized person in some respects, and that makes life harder than it has to be," admits Bateman. "Amanda is quite particular and inflexible in her work approach; she has had to try and be more open to different, new, and potentially better ways of doing things and not stress the small stuff.

"We've learned that we each have our strengths in the business, whether in administration, running the kitchen, running the floor, dealing with customers, managing staff, and so on. As we identify these strengths, we're getting better at dividing our work accordingly, and not being so critical of the other person if they're not 100 percent perfect in all areas at all times.

"We've also learned that we're remarkably good at working together, and we're grateful that we still want to spend much of our 'downtime' with each other, despite spending a crazy amount of each day in close proximity!" says Bateman.

Relationship with Staff

Depending on the type of business you're in, when you're first starting out, the temptation is to bootstrap to save money and do everything yourself. This may work for a short time, but if you want your business to grow, eventually, you're going to need help in the form of paid employees.

"You could be a one-person band and perform in the subways, but if you want to get out there and perform in stadiums, you're going to need some help," says Main Street Vegan Academy's Victoria Moran.

Her thoughts are echoed by Alicia Lai, owner of Bourgeois Boheme, a luxury shoe brand in London. "You have to understand that you're not superwoman or superman. You might want to do everything, but you've got to say, 'Okay, I have limitations, but I have positives too.' So really work on what your strengths are and try and get people to help with the other aspects of the business," says Lai.

Hypnotherapist, naturopath, and business mindset coach Dr Tracie O'Keefe's motto is to accentuate your best and delegate the rest.

"I've grown my business to a level where my staff handle much of the day-to-day administration that would distract me from helping people with their health and training their minds. I studied for decades to hone my skills and focus my energies on helping people change the way their mind works to be successful in life and business. Know what you're good at in business, study it, and practice it until you're an expert. Focus on what you do to make money and outsource the rest. Don't struggle to do what you're not talented at doing," says O'Keefe.

Attracting and retaining motivated, honest, and reliable staff begins with you. An ethical leader isn't domineering, but, instead, helps others to be innovative and to lead. Communication, again, is key here.

"You need to teach people how to help you," says Fry's Family Foods's Wally Fry. "Being patient and repeating yourself a lot comes with the territory when you have a vision that others don't initially share. Don't just expect people to buy into your dream. You have to teach them your dream and your standards so they can live your legacy."

Jewelry maker Ele Keats agrees. "It's your responsibility to hire people who reflect you and to train them in how you want them to represent your brand," she says.

Finding the right staff can be a challenge, particularly in the hospitality sector. As 222 Veggie Vegan's Ben Asamani points out: "Many people today just want a job to earn some money, so nothing drives them, and that's a challenge I face a lot in running a vegan business. Because I own the restaurant, I make sure things are done to the standard that I believe is right. Most businesses employ someone who doesn't really care, so, sometimes, it might get very challenging in the kitchen," says Asamani.

Sometimes it can be difficult to find staff with similar values in a particular geographical area, as is the case for Rubyfruit café in the Blue Mountains area of New South Wales, Australia. "Staffing is extremely difficult for us," reveals Simone Bateman. "Hospitality is a transient industry, and we're located in a regional area with a limited pool of vegan or vegetarian hospitality professionals to draw from. We advertise on Facebook, in the local paper, and in relevant vegan forums, but there are simply not enough qualified people around."

Despite the challenges, it's possible to have employees so content that, like Disney's Seven Dwarfs, they whistle while they work, or, in the case of Wellinhand, sing. "My staff sing all day," laughs owner Linda Doby. "It's hilarious, the things that they do, and they just find joy in it all."

Doby attributes this phenomenally happy work culture to allowing staff to have flexible hours and honoring their lives outside work. "Everybody is part time. I work around their schedules, give or take, and I'm very flexible *all* the time. Then when a big order comes up, they rise to the occasion and they pull it out of their hats because they know that I've been flexible forever. Everybody has a 'pitch-in' attitude. Recently we had a huge pallet to pack for this particular order, and we were really excited because it was a long time coming. We had quite a bit to figure out and they just took the reins and were so co-operative; it was great and fun to watch," says Doby.

In addition to allowing flexible hours, including staff in the company's decisions is another reason Doby, whose longest-serving employee has been with her 17 years out of 20, cites for their commitment. "You've got to listen to their ideas because I don't just hire them for their hands; I hire their heads too. It doesn't matter if they're new, I still hire their brains. Truthfully, the ones who are happiest are going to be the ones who are thinkers, conjurers, and problem-solvers," says Doby.

Justin Mead, co-owner of Vegan Style, a shoe store in Melbourne, Australia, takes a similar approach. Two of his staff are university students, and, if the store is quiet, he allows them time to catch up on their studies. He also includes staff in key decisions and utilizes all their skills. "If we have a new supplier, I get their opinion on how we should proceed, and, if so, with what styles. One of my staff is a great writer, so I ask her to help with newsletters, and another employee is a photographer. If they get to use their other skills, it keeps them engaged," says Mead.

Grace Love, owner of Bliss Organic Café in Adelaide, South Australia, also offers a flexible approach to staff hours. "For those employees who require stability, they have the guarantee of set, regular hours. And for those who like flexibility, they can opt for casual hours or be on call," says Love.

Treating staff fairly and compensating them satisfactorily is the bare minimum that vegan business owners should strive for. Lagusta Yearwood of Lagusta's Luscious chocolate store recommends going way beyond the basics when it comes to employees. "Our philosophy is to absolutely slather our staff with kindness, perks, good wages, and autonomy. We make it very clear to them how essential they are to us, and, in return, we expect loyalty and energy and an excellent work ethic," she says. The result is an "incredibly low turnover rate."

If you're able to, paying staff over and above the going rate is a good strategy to engender loyalty and get employees to care about the business enough to want it to succeed. Lee Coates of Ethical Investors and Cruelty Free Super has found this to be the case.

"We are more successful because we've got staff not just saying, '5, 4, 3, 2, 1, home time—I'm out the door.' Instead they say, 'I'll just get that job finished before I go home because I know I'm respected for what I do and I'm paid well for what I do, so I'll just give a little bit back to the business.' It's a virtuous circle. If you work for an employer who will screw you down to the lowest possible wage, then you'll be out that door.

"My staff make sure that all the computer screens, computers, and photocopiers are switched off at the end of the day because they know it saves the business money and it's the right thing to do, whereas if you work for an employer who has no respect for you, when it comes time to go home, you walk out the door; it's not a problem if the photocopier is left on all night. If it's left on all night, that's burning electricity, which costs the business money, but you don't pay your staff well enough for them to care whether it costs the business money, so the business is less profitable. These little things build up, and turning off the machines makes the business more profitable," says Coates.

Even if you can't pay your staff over and above financially, there are other ways to make them feel valued. Ms. Cupcake's Mellissa Morgan advocates treating your staff like family, taking care of your team, and including them in decisions about the business. "I meet with each staff member on a one-to-one basis once a month for them to talk about the key question: 'What would you do to make this business better?' Because they can come up with some golden stuff. They are the best people at your fingertips, and you need to start listening to them as a business owner to help yourself grow.

"We can't pay huge sums of money because our profit margins are so slim, so I go out of my way to find different ways to ensure that my team knows they are valued. Like we closed the shop two hours early recently because the staff had a couple of really busy weeks, and I needed to take them out for dinner to say 'thank you.' Sometimes, it's about putting the business second and putting your team first," says Morgan.

This is an important point. As David Benzaquen from Plant-Based Solutions notes, too often, mission-driven groups such as vegan business owners believe that because we, as founders, are willing to sacrifice any creature comforts and throw 100 percent of our time into our companies, everyone else should have to do the same. "We are all more effective when we have our essential physical and emotional needs met," says Benzaquen.

Vegan Mainstream's Stephanie Redcross agrees and emphasizes the importance of not burning out your staff.

"As owners, we put our lives, our souls—everything—into our businesses. Yet, for employees, it's not the same thing. Even if they're passionate, it can't be on the same level. So we have to be very careful about expecting our employees to live and breathe our businesses. The responsibility is on us to avoid burning our employees out and to recognize that, sometimes, we have to give them permission to log off. It's important to notice when they're working too much, and to say something at those times. It's vital to always make them feel appreciated. And if they're going on vacation, it will serve you well to give them space and say, 'I'm not going to bother you. I'm not going to email you unless it's an emergency,'" says Redcross.

She also advises against sending emails to staff in the middle of the night. "As the business owner, you need to ensure that people don't become guilty or feel like they're slacking if they don't respond immediately to an email that you sent at 2am. Sending emails at this time suggests that you want them to be up in the middle of the night," says Redcross.

Another reason employees may get burned out is if they're pigeon-holed into one particular aspect of work and become bored and disheartened. Integrating your staff into various parts of your business can do a lot to avoid this.

"If you have people who are in the warehouse, consider bringing them into a marketing think tank," says Redcross. "Or if you have some amazing warehouse workers, feature them on your social media site. Don't just feature yourself or the PR person. Put others out there and say, 'This is the person who packs your bags,' or, 'This is the person who allows us to have accuracy on all of our shipping,' or, 'This is the person in operations who came up with this great idea.' Positive public recognition is a powerful motivator for staff because they realize they're not just the best kept secret; you're bragging to the world that they're amazing."

Bringing staff into key decisions also helps to make them feel valued. "If you're going to bring them into things like think-tank discussions, incorporate their ideas. This doesn't mean that everyone gets to vote on *everything* in your company. But try to shake things up! When you're making decisions on packaging, for example, consider asking people who aren't in the market-ing department what they think. Remember, all your employees represent your business, your brand and—especially if they've been with you for a while—they may have valuable ideas to con-tribute. Ask their perspective. This is a good way to show people that they're valued outside of just one skill set," says Redcross.

Iku franchisee Kendall Hayes does right by her staff by giv-ing them autonomy and flexibility. "I think they appreciate the trust we place in them. We are mindful that food service is prob-ably not their ultimate career, so we give our staff flexibility for holidays and study. They've told us that we inspire them with our lifestyle, and many of them are now on their own health journeys, which includes exploring a plant-based diet," says Hayes.

One of the best ways to attract staff is to create a brand that people believe is so wonderful that they clamor to work for you, as they do with Google and Apple. Within the vegan business market, Veggie Grill, Plamil Foods, and Bliss Organic Café have no shortage of people wanting to secure employment with the companies.

"First and foremost, our differentiation is that we are something that people can really feel good about," says Veggie Grill's T.K. Pillan. "A lot of people want to be involved because they do feel that we are making a difference. They're attracted to what we stand for, so that allows us to both attract and keep good people."

Plamil Foods in the UK has the added benefit of being a chocolate factory and an ethical one to boot, which, together with a pleasant and positive working environment, goes a long way to explaining why most of the just under 50 employees tend to stay at the company long term.

"It's a 24-hour, seven-days-a-week operation, and we tend to find when we recruit people that if they last more than a few weeks, they're with us for a long, long time," says managing director Adrian Ling. "If you create interest in the job, give staff ownership of the job, and allow them to input ideas, they can grow with the company. It's very rare that we lose somebody who has been with us for any length of time."

In South Australia, Grace Love receives around 10 resumés every week for Bliss Organic Café positions, which she attributes to the business being unique, vegan, and in a location frequented by Adelaide's local vegan population as well as visitors to the city.

If you're fortunate enough to be in the position of having people queuing up to work for you, it helps to eliminate those who are simply seeking a job, although you still have to be sure that the person is a good fit for your company, is passionate about it, and can communicate your values.

The Cruelty Free Shop's Jessica Bailey looks for personality over experience. "I don't advertise for staff because I'm too concerned that customers will apply, not get the job, and get annoyed, so it's always just through friends. One of our staff members is an ex-customer who used to come in all the time and one day just said, 'Are you looking for anyone?' And they were just the right type of person. We hire purely based on personality because anyone can learn how to use a tool or pack an order. It's about who fits with the team and their passion for veganism. It's important to me that if a customer who's thinking of becoming vegan comes into the shop and asks questions, the person answering them needs to be really passionate about it. The staff are told that if someone like that comes into the shop, give them all the time they need."

Addiction Food's Georgie Campbell takes a similar approach. "We look for someone *really* positive and personally motivated— happy not just for the interview but generally in life. We go in with the right attitude and we train them. But staff need to take ownership of their work and be accountable for it. There is a great team culture, and we get them involved in our business. We give them that responsibility and they love it, and we generally know straightaway if they're going to fit," says Campbell.

Despite their challenges of finding staff in their local area, Rubyfruit owners Amanda Solomons and Simone Bateman go all out to find the right person. "We design our ads to attract people who are not only experienced but also want to change the world through vegan food," says Bateman. "When we do find the right staff, we do our best to keep them keen, motivated, and positive by offering a passionate, honest, and fun team environment. We also offer opportunities for advancement wherever we can, to keep people challenged, interested, and satisfied by their work. We have such a small team that we generally end up close friends, which can be both a blessing and a challenge. Our staff have got to believe in our business, in what we're doing, or it doesn't work."

One of the mistakes business owners make when seeking employees is expecting every staff member to be perfect. "We found hiring our first staff members a little stressful as we were looking for the 'perfect' person, but we learned fairly quickly that each person has strengths and weaknesses," says Iku's Kendall Hayes. "It's about building a team that works well together and it's up to us to bring out the best in everyone."

Jivamukti Yoga's Sharon Gannon agrees. "It's rare that you have the perfect people surrounding you. We don't blame other people for not being as passionate as we are. We have got to continue on, hope for the best, love them and be compassionate toward them, and, hopefully, by example, they might feel that they could be more on board with our values. Usually, we encourage that life is short and that people should do what moves them, what feeds their passion. So, if our message of spirituality, veganism, animal rights, and political activism doesn't really move them, then, usually, those employees don't last that long," says Gannon.

If you can't yet afford local staff, there are ways to get creative. Calling on friends or family members to help you out occasionally is one. This can have a bonus impact, as Vegan Proteins's Dani Taylor found out. "We have one office worker, my sister. We try to keep as much business in the family as we're able to. This has helped our families shift toward veganism, when that was never even a possibility before," says Taylor.

Internships are another way to get expert help, either for free or a low fee. However, while this can be a win-win, with the interns gaining valuable work experience, it's important for you, as an ethical business owner, not to exploit them. A short-term arrangement where the intern works a few hours a week unpaid is one thing, but expecting them to work full time over a long period with no wages is unfair and unethical. It could even result in legal action against you.

Even if you can't afford to pay interns a wage, covering their travel expenses and providing meals for them if they're working at your location is recommended, along with giving them proper breaks throughout the day. Make sure you also train them and give them tasks that stretch and engage them. Sending them on the coffee or lunch run or getting them to file paperwork is fine; just don't make these their only jobs.

Nowadays, as we live and operate in a global marketplace, it's possible to hire staff from other countries at far lower rates than you'd need to pay locally. You can get a full-time virtual assistant (a personal assistant who works remotely) for 40 hours a week for less than a daily rate for a local person. Of course, there are pros and cons, and it may not be a fit for your business. If you do go down this route, be considerate of the staff members' needs and lives outside of working with you. Many live in countries where there are regular earthquakes, cyclones, hurricanes, and storms that devastate their homes and lives.

Information on hiring a virtual assistant from overseas can be found at **www.veganbusinessmedia.com/resources**

Bartering goods and services is another way to get work done without outlaying cash.

"We've become savvy about bartering with other people for their time because when you don't have money, you can't afford to hire a PR or a marketing professional," says Vegan Proteins's Giacomo Marchese. "So you learn how to help others and have them help you. Because, let's face it, we all get very busy as adults and none of us have the time, but when you find something that someone else really wants and vice versa, you find a way to fit that into your schedule. Because we also provide personal training, we have a couple of friends who we train for free, and they, in turn, help promote us."

Victoria Moran utilizes a similar approach, occasionally allowing a student traveling to New York to attend the Main Street Vegan Academy course to trade services as Moran's assistant and stay with her to avoid paying hotel costs.

If you have any doubts about the investment of time or expenditure in staff and the need to treat them well, take heed of this advice from publicist Kezia Jauron, co-owner of Evolotus PR in

Los Angeles: "Employers need to value their employees, and for-profit businesses, vegan or not, need to pay a competitive wage and treat their employees humanely. Departing staff shouldn't be given any reason to vent on social media or to friends about how awful you are to work for," says Jauron.

Relationship with Consultants and Other Professionals

In addition to staff, you'll likely require the services of other professionals. These could be business coaches, media coaches, marketing and PR experts, project managers, or mentors. Again, you'll need to cultivate strong relationships with these professionals to encourage and inspire them to go all out for your business success. If they genuinely care about you and your values and you develop a mutual trust and rapport, they'll become your advocates.

"I couldn't have grown my business to where it is now without a coach," says image consultant Ginger Burr. "It's so easy to doubt myself or go into a place of 'what ifs,' but having someone to bounce ideas off, help get my psychic energy back where it needs to be, or push me and support me to go further has been invaluable. My current business coach has helped me create systems in my business that add value for my clients and keep me sane, which is so important. In one and a half years, I doubled my income. I never could have done that on my own."

The Veggie Grill team brought in a group of experts, both when starting out and to expand their chain of restaurants. They formed a Board of Advisers initially comprising two experienced restaurant partners who helped get the chain up to seven outlets. After that, they sought out senior people who had grown national restaurant chains to help the company figure out how to go from being a regional chain to becoming a national one.

"You've got to surround yourself with people who have the same purpose and values and complementary skill sets," says T.K. Pillan. "That, I think, has been the biggest key to our success at

Veggie Grill. What we've done is bring on the right people at the right time with the right skill sets but also a shared purpose and common set of values. We would prepare a status on the business and details of everything that was going on, and the Board of Advisers gave us great advice based on their years of experience."

As we saw in Chapter 2 in the case of The Cruelty Free Shop's Jessica Bailey, having a business mentor to give you a reality check and guide you can be the difference between your business succeeding or failing.

Truth Belts owner Renia Pruchnicki has benefited from hiring business consultants. "I was working so much in my business, doing the hands-on stuff that I couldn't see what was going on. The consultants came in to help me, and I realized I had to make some changes if I wanted to grow. Having business mentors who are successful to help you see your business in a different light is really important," says Pruchnicki.

You must, however, choose the right consultant.

Stephanie Redcross notes it's crucial that the professional help you hire understands your market. "A lot of times, advisers have great suggestions. But if they don't understand the vegan market—and when I say 'the vegan market' I don't mean just vegans, I mean people consuming vegan products or services—they'll miss the mark. It's not because they're bad marketers or advisers; it's just that they're not focused. It doesn't mean they have to be vegan or vegetarian, but they have to understand the vegan market, your industry, and what you're doing," says Redcross.

As well as understanding your market and industry, a professional must know how to work with you at your level. Someone who's worked only for large corporate firms may not understand how a small business operates. "You have to make sure you're going to work with someone who knows what it's like to work with a small team where there are three core people, plus part-time, freelance, or remote staff," says Redcross. "You're *not* an 18-person business, you're really three with a support team around you, and you need to be working with somebody who understands that dynamic. Otherwise, they may put too much weight on your small business when coming up with marketing ideas and strategies, which—no matter how good the ideas are—can do more harm than good if you can't handle the recommendations."

So when should you hire professional help, especially if you're already stretching your budget?

Speaker and executive coach Ron Prasad says many new business owners go into business without thinking much about marketing in terms of the time and money that it will require. "You can ask yourself the question: 'Do I have more time or more money?' If you have more time, then do research on marketing. Study the materials of experts such as Dan Kennedy, Mal Emery, and Seth Godin. Implement what they suggest," says Prasad.

When hiring a consultant to help you with your business, Prasad recommends asking the person a series of questions.

"Whenever I am approached by a potential client, one of the things that I offer them is the contact details of any two of my past or present clients. I strongly suggest that they contact these two individuals to ask about me and my services."

In addition to asking potential consultants' past or present client contact information, Prasad suggests asking the person questions such as:

- What has been your experience in working with businesses like mine?
- How likely are we to achieve the goals that we have discussed?
- What is your philosophy when coaching/mentoring a client?
- What types of measurable results have you helped your clients achieve?
- Do you offer a satisfaction guarantee of some type?

"Interview two or three consultants, coaches, or experts before you make a decision. Ask yourself, 'Do I feel a connection with this person?'" says Prasad.

On the flip side, you, as the business owner, also need to be coachable and prepared to take on the advice of the professional. The interview is a two-way process, says Prasad. "Be it life coaching or business coaching, I am emphatic in telling my clients from the onset, one simple truth: 'A fitness trainer won't go down and do the push ups for you.' Likewise, I don't do the work for my clients. I'll give them advice and it's up to them to implement the advice. Yes, I'll hold them accountable and give them 'homework.' But it's up to them to do the 'homework.' Between sessions, I check up on my clients to see how things are going. Their level of commitment is something that I'm very particular with. If I feel that they're dipping their toes in too many ponds, I won't take them on as a client. I look for focus in a potential client," says Prasad.

We'll cover hiring PR and marketing professionals in more detail in the chapters on marketing later in this book.

Relationship with Customers

Your relationship with your potential and existing customers is, of course, paramount to the success of your business. While this has always been the case, it's even more pertinent nowadays with online review sites and social media, where people can make public comments about you and your business. As consumers, we're swayed by both positive and negative feedback we see online. It's not what *you* say about yourself or your business that counts, it's what others are saying. Potential customers give more weight to the latter.

Excellent customer service is essential because people buy based on how you (or your product/service) make them *feel*. Yes, you must have outstanding quality products or services, but without a fantastic customer experience, consumers will buy your competitors' equally outstanding product or service (they may even buy a still good-quality but slightly inferior product or service if the competitor's customer service blows yours out of the water).

"In Western society, customer service is dying," says Prasad. "If you are to stand out, I suggest that you start off with customer service. According to statistics, the average unhappy client will tell between nine and 11 people, who, in turn, will tell a further six to seven individuals each—which could be 60 people who probably won't use you."

Vegan Proteins's Dani Taylor highlights the importance of raving fans and word-of-mouth referrals, which can save a ton of money on advertising and marketing costs. "We almost don't even have to promote ourselves in the large vegan fitness groups online, because other people do it for us," says Taylor.

Many business owners become angry and upset at critical, negative feedback, but the fact a customer takes the time to provide feedback is actually gold for you. It can be hard eliciting feedback from clients—those of you who have asked your clientele to fill out a short survey, even enticing them with a gift for participating, know that getting customers to take the time to do this is difficult, even if they're happy with your services.

So, when a customer takes the time to leave a negative comment on social media or online review site, don't go into a tizzy. Reframe the situation and be grateful for the feedback and the opportunity to improve your customer experience.

Nikki Medwell, owner of Australia's first vegan bed and breakfast in Victoria, takes customer feedback seriously. "We put a feedback form in the room for each guest, and we absorbed every piece of feedback we got—everything. Anytime someone suggested something, we'd implement it. We had this big guy staying once and we had a shower curtain instead of a glass screen. He wrote on the form that the shower curtain stuck to him and said, 'I felt like I was doing the dance of the seven veils in the shower; it was uncomfortable for me.' So we immediately had someone come and put in glass screen doors," says Medwell.

Letting clients know that you have implemented their feedback is also an excellent customer service strategy. "We responded by email to every person, whether they gave good, bad, or indifferent feedback, and 90 percent of them would reply, saying, 'Thank you so much for acknowledging that or for letting us know why something was the way it was,'" says Medwell.

Rubyfruit's Amanda Solomons and Simone Bateman also take on customer feedback, which has resulted in the creation of new menu innovations. "We regularly engage our customers, both in person and on social media, in ideas for new product lines, flavors and menu changes. We note their feedback, take it on board, and adjust our approach accordingly, without losing our core values or business model," says Bateman.

"Customers wanted fast lunches they could grab in a hurry. So we now prepare ready-made wraps and salads that can be purchased 'on the run.' When the weather cooled down, customers wanted quick, take-away meals that were warming. We purchased a bain marie and soup kettle, and developed a hot 'In a Hurry?' lunch menu. And when we noted that more and more customers were asking to buy meals cold to take away to heat for dinner, we started packaging ready-made meals that are now available fresh or frozen for easy at-home dinners."

Ensuring her customers get exquisite quality products along with excellent service is a priority for Sandy Anderson, owner of Veganpet, an Australian wet and dry human-grade, vet-approved, scientifically evaluated dog and cat food. So determined is she to provide potential customers with such high quality and service that she will even decline sales.

"Even though Veganpet has been clinically tested and I can put my money where my mouth is, if a customer tells me their animal has a urinary problem or something, I will say that the cat or dog shouldn't go on my food," says Anderson. "I tell them if their vet is happy, then maybe we can come across to Veganpet. Their vet has got to be involved. Then I speak to the vet and I send them all the data that they need, and, sometimes, they come back and say, 'No, I'm sorry, this cat is on a prescription diet and can't go off it.' My customers are fabulous, but some of them get so stubborn about wanting their cat or dog on Veganpet. I try to make them understand that, sometimes, you just can't do it."

Another example of outstanding customer service is demonstrated by Candle Cafe's Joy Pierson and Bart Potenza, who enabled a young boy to have his first ever birthday cake. "He's in college now, but, at the time, he was eight and had all these food allergies, including dairy, nuts, and gluten," explains Potenza. "Because of the high standards our chefs have, we were able to make a cake for him. We even got him special chocolate chips from Israel that had never even touched a dairy-making machine."

It's this kind of dedication to the customer experience that encourages loyalty and support to a brand, even during economic downturns—something Ben Asamani has experienced. "Even though some people were going through financial difficulty in the Global Financial Crisis in 2008, they still wanted to eat something healthy and delicious. There are customers who love this place so much that they don't want it to close down, so sometimes they say, 'Let's go out and support 222 Veggie Vegan,'" says Asamani.

As well as developing excellent relationships with potential and existing clients in person or via your own website and customer relationship management systems, social media plays a key role. We'll look at this in more detail in the chapter on social media marketing, but the important thing to remember is that social media are platforms you should use to build trust and create communities of people who love your brand. It's not the place to do "hard sell." And you need to be patient.

"A lot of business owners think that they're going to share a link online and then that's going to go viral and sell a heap of things," says Australian-based social media consultant Leigh-

Chantelle. "But that just doesn't happen anymore, and the whole idea with social media marketing is creating your tribe online, and, to do that, that you need to create trust."

You can't have too many customer testimonials, so do solicit and encourage them. Check out this article I wrote on the Vegan Business Media website: "How to Ask for a Testimonial That Will Serve Your vegan Business": **www.veganbusinessmedia.com/how-to-ask-for-a-testimonial-that-will-serve-your-vegan-business-2**

Relationship with Suppliers, Wholesalers, Retailers, Manufacturers

What other services you need to run your business efficiently and successfully will depend on the type of business. Pretty much all businesses will need a website nowadays, so a freelance web designer and developer (who may or may not be the same person) is likely to be part of your team.

The same goes for business cards, so finding a good printer is important, particularly if you're looking at getting flyers, brochures, portable banners for events, and other materials.

If you outsource the manufacturing, packing, and distribution of your products to enable your business to grow, you must have impeccable relationships with these people, as they're responsible for how your customers experience your brand. If your product arrives late or damaged in a ripped packet, this reflects directly on you and your brand.

If you're dealing with wholesalers and retailers, again, the quality of your relationship with them is crucial. "At the end of the day, retailers run a commercial business, and, if they're going to take a leap of faith and stock a new brand or a new line of products or start to cater to the vegan market, then they need to know that those products are going to be around long term," says Vegan Perfection's Jeremy Johnson.

"If a product or brand disappears after six months, and they've devoted their shelf space to it and given time to develop the product or brand, that's probably the worst thing that can happen for a retailer. If this happens, then they have empty shelf space they need to fill with another product that they'll need to establish all over again, which takes time and costs money. It's rare that a product will just fly straight off the shelves the minute it's introduced; it's usually a bit of a slow burn. You have to convince retailers that you're going to be around long enough that they're going to have a long, successful relationship with you, and with your products."

Johnson experienced first hand what happens when suppliers and others in the chain let you down after his first shipment of perishable stock from the UK to Australia was ruined because it was left out in the open at Dubai airport. "That was one of the biggest challenges we have ever faced, right as we were starting our business, but we managed to just survive," he says. "It goes back to that relationship that we build with retailers and with the people who consume our products. They expect a steady supply of the product and they expect it to be in good condition and of high quality. Even if we have suppliers letting us down or we have freight-forwarders or people involved in the logistical side of the business letting us down, our customers and retailers expect us to find a solution to these problems. Such problems will pass on directly to our customers and our retailers if a solution isn't found."

In Johnson's case, because Vegan Perfection only supplies to smaller, independent stores, rather than big supermarket chains, the people at those stores were more understanding, but "their patience only extends so far", he says.

Relationship with Collaborators and Competitors
You may wonder why I've put both collaborators and competitors in the same section, instead of separating them. The reason is that the new way of doing business, particularly in the ethical space, involves treating your competitors as collaborators.

So, instead of thinking in terms of how you can "crush it" in your industry or "kill" your competitors in a "war" for customers, you reframe your language and approach from violence to compassion. When done well, this strategy can result in a win-win for everyone, instead of the typical win-lose scenario entrenched in traditional business models.

Author and vegan lifestyle coach JL Fields took the initiative in creating a collaboration between her and three newly qualified vegan lifestyle coaches from her local area in Colorado Springs. In 2014, Fields, who is on the faculty at Victoria Moran's Main Street Vegan Academy, was faced with training what some may have seen as potential competitors to her business, and used this to teach a smart lesson to all 15 trainees in the room.

"I said to them, 'Some of you might think that you're going back and you're going to be competitive with people. I'm training three people in front of me right now who are going back to my town. And you know what I'm going to do? I'm going to ask them what their focus is going to be. What are they really good at? How do they want to work with people? What do they want to do?'" explains Fields.

At the end of the training, Fields gathered the three trainees, along with Moran, and got a photo taken of the group. She then instructed the newly qualified "competitors" to send her their biographies, their website URLs, and details of their coaching philosophy. It turned out one coach's philosophy was around the environment, another was around mind, body, and wellness, and the third one was an athlete. Fields's speciality is home cooking.

Fields then sent a press release to her local newspaper, along with the group photo and biographies, along the theme of 'How lucky are we! Colorado Springs now has four vegan lifestyle coaches—meet them.' In the release, she described each of them.

"You know what happens when you build that collaboration? It's really hard to look at one another as competitors," says Fields. "Instead, what happens is, if someone came to me and said, 'I want vegan lifestyle coaching and I want to do an ironman,' I'd say, 'You need to talk to Matt because Matt is an ironman.' If they want to reduce their carbon footprint, I tell them to talk to Sarah. And if they want to make meals with five ingredients or less, then I'm their girl."

Competition forces you to be honest with yourself about what you're actually good at, says Fields. "A lot of times, people think they can do everything. It's that 'pick me, pick me!' attitude. Well, can you really do everything? Or can you do all of them sort of well but two things expertly? Why not just focus on things that you're great at and pass on the rest to the other person who's an expert at two things you're not great at? You become collaborators and not competitors," says Fields.

Vegan Proteins's Dani Taylor, who also works as a personal trainer, embraces this collaborative approach. "If I have a coaching client come to me, and I think they would be a better fit for Vegan Muscle and Fitness, for example, I'll send them over there, and vice versa. When you have these relationships with similar-but-different types of businesses and organizations and you go out of your way to help each other out, it comes back to you two-fold. Everyone benefits, and the vegan message spreads further. It's a win-win," says Taylor.

This kind of collaborative approach isn't limited to coaches. Veggie Grill recommends other vegan eateries to customers, provided they offer a different dining experience. "Anybody who's focused on the veggie space from a food product standpoint is a potential collaborator. We support and recommend other veggie-based restaurants around town because they offer slightly different things than we do," says T.K. Pillan.

Skincare expert Samantha Crosby from Ayana Organics sees everyone spreading the vegan message as a potential collaborator, rather than competitor. "We've been involved in several collaborations. For example, I guest blog for other likeminded businesses and they return with a blog post for our site. We also collaborate with an Australian author. We promote her book and she promotes our products. I see collaborations as a very effective way to increase exposure and send out collective messages," says Crosby.

Tofurky's Seth Tibbott also values competitors, referring to them as "a tide that lifts all boats." "If you have a category in a store, let's say diapers, and diapers are hot and growing and people are innovating and the category is supercharged, it's easier for you to take your new diaper and get placement on the shelf," he explains. "But if the category is shrinking and not doing so well, then the space in the store shrinks and you come in with your innovative diaper and the store says, 'We have enough already, thank you. We don't need that.' So we try to look at competition as opportunity for us and as a positive thing because if you drink beer or wine, you rarely would buy the same beer or wine all the time or eat the same breakfast cereal or whatever, so it's healthy to have competitors," says Tibbott.

The Cruelty Free Shop's Jessica Bailey admits she was initially troubled by competitors who came after her, but quickly learned to embrace them as collaborators. "When I first started the online store, we were the only one, and a few years after that, there were two other people who started up very similar online stores. At first, I was like, 'How could they? This is terrible! There's not enough vegans to go around!'" she says, laughing. "And then I thought, 'Maybe there *are* enough vegans to go around, in which case, that's great, because it means the vegan population is growing. And since then, I realized that the more vegan businesses there are, the better, because that fits in with our goal to make vegan products more readily available. So now, every time a new business opens, I embrace it and send them congratulatory emails. I'd much rather be competing with other vegan businesses than huge supermarkets or non-vegan businesses, and there is room; the vegan market is growing, so there's room for others," says Bailey.

Iku Wholefood's Ken Israel agrees. "In the early days, I'd

become a bit fearful of competition, but when I think about it, my initial motivation was to have better quality food out there, and what better way to do it than have other people doing it? So, the more people do it, the better," he says. "I drive up the coast and I see replicas of our product everywhere, and I used to think, 'Geez, they're ripping us off.' But now I think, 'Wow, that's fantastic!'"

Of course if someone does steal your intellectual property to make a lower-quality replica of your product, you may need to take legal action. But, as Mai Lieu, author of *Take the Next Step*, notes, your best recourse is to come out with a better, more innovative product to re-establish customer loyalty.

Some vegan business owners go beyond collaboration to establishing friendships with their competitors.

"I refuse to not be friends with the other vegan businesses doing chocolate and pastry work," says Lagusta Yearwood. "The market is so big and life is too short. It's fun to see what your 'competitors' are doing, and, as someone who started out in life as an animal rights activist, I just can't think ill of a vegan who's devoted their life to advancing veganism."

Ms. Cupcake's Mellissa Morgan lives by a similar philosophy. "I don't mind the competition because even if 50 people started vegan cupcake businesses in the same area of London as I am, there would be 50 different businesses because they're run by 50 different people, and I find comfort in that," she says.

Morgan shares business with and is friends with other vegan cupcake makers, a move that benefits all involved. "My feeling always was if I make friends with my potential competitors or my actual competitors, we're far more likely to not step on each other's toes if we know each other, and this has actually rung really, really true," she says.

"I've found some amazing other business owners that do similar things to what we do and we pass business back and forth between each other. If I'm busy and can't take on any more orders, I'll pass it on to a different business that I think might be able to take it, and it comes the other way around as well. This way, we're helping each other's businesses to grow rather than being like some cutthroat competition," says Morgan.

Truth Belts owner Renia Pruchnicki is inspired, rather than threatened, by her competitors. "My competitors have influenced me and inspired me to do something wonderful because we're all doing something that's wonderful for the planet, so I don't have any hard feelings for my competitors. I'd love to meet with them and go out for dinner!" she chuckles.

Some owners of vegan-run businesses do invite their competitors—vegan or otherwise—to dinner or lunch. "When I started, people were telling me, 'Oh, Grace, this place is a competitor.' I said, 'Come on, let's just invite everyone for lunch for free and we'll have fun,'" says Bliss Organic Café's Grace Love. "It's all about working together because if someone else has vegan options as well but they might have something we don't have, we always send customers over to the other shop, and they send customers over to us. I believe working together takes us further than working against each other, and I always say, the more vegan places, the better."

Cruelty Free Super's Lee Coates meets up with a senior representative of a rival 'ethical' (non-vegan) superannuation fund each time he visits Australia. "We catch up to see what each other is up to," says Coates. "Cruelty Free Super is gradually no longer seen as the new kid on the block. The other fund is in their ethical space, and we're in our cruelty-free space. The more the ethical market gets bigger, the better it is for all of us. We're collaborating to increase the size of our particular market, and, as this happens, the customers can choose which bit of the market most appeals to them."

Collaborating with other vegan-run businesses can be cost-effective too. As we noted in the previous chapter, the cost of materials or ingredients is higher when bought in small quantities. So, working with other businesses to bulk buy these items results in a benefit for each business.

Cow Jones Industrials's Donna Oakes-Jones proposed the idea of an ethical shop guild to business owners. "In order to be part of this guild, the majority of the products sold by each business would have to fit into different categories: vegan/ sustainable materials/fair labor/local artists. We discussed approaching designers to see if we could somehow share minimum orders. We also discussed the possibility of working with each other to ensure that we didn't carry the same styles by the same designers to try to give each of us some type of exclusivity," says Oakes-Jones.

The Regal Vegan's Ella Nemcova collaborated to get vegan booths at the popular outdoor, all-food, hipster Smorgasburg markets in Brooklyn, New York. Hers was the first vegan booth, which was challenging, as not many vegans were coming to the markets because of a lack of vegan booths.

As a couple more came on board, the businesses made a decision to embrace and support each other. "We tweeted and we supported each other through multiple media campaigns, putting out the message of, 'We're all here. We have vegan booths now; there are four vegan booths, there are five vegan booths now. We are growing, and we need you to come.' And the vegans came because there was something to come to," says Nemcova.

Iku Wholefood's Kendall Hayes recently partnered with some small local vegan food businesses to expand her branch's offerings. "Everyone has something unique to offer. It's a win-win situation, as we get to offer exciting new products to our customers, while helping small ethical businesses to expand their reach in a market that's becoming increasingly saturated," she says.

While collaboration with other vegan businesses is a win for everyone, so too can teaming up with local non-vegan businesses.

The Cruelty Free Shop's Jessica Bailey created an annual Vegan Day Out in the Sydney and Melbourne suburbs where her stores are located. She contacts local businesses and encourages them to offer additional vegan options and/or discounts on their existing vegan offerings. It brings more vegans into the area to visit her shop as well as the added attraction of other offerings from other businesses. And the other businesses get to see the rise in vegan clientele.

If you're bristling at the thought of helping non-vegan businesses to make money, remember that in late 2014, GustOrganics in New York announced it was becoming a vegan restaurant to save the planet. The restaurant got quite a bit of flack from paleo advocates and lost a lot of customers (Goldensohn, 2015). The owners stuck to their decision and by early 2015 the restaurant's entire menu became vegan. If our aim is for vegan world domination, encouraging non-vegan businesses to convert must be on our agenda.

In the UK, Kevin Newell, owner of Humane Wildlife Solutions, collaborates with other businesses that fit with his values, even if they're not vegan.

"We believe working together with others is a vital tool for helping wildlife," he says. "We would never work with another 'pest control business' as they're all lethal businesses killing wildlife. However, we do work with the likes of the fox specialists who are non-lethal in the London and Kent areas. We often send work to each other if we have jobs in areas that the other businesses cover. Sharing ideas and jobs helps us all to continue our important work."

Bed and Broccoli's Nikki Medwell reached out to local suppliers in the rural, dairy bowl area she lives in when she was unable to find vegan versions. "I was forced to make a lot of things that I would normally buy, whether sour crème, for instance, or vegan feta. I was able to strike up a good relationship with the local store manager who offered to stock any ingredients I needed," says Medwell, who scored a monthly recipe column in her local paper. "They publish my recipes and I can now say, 'You can buy this ingredient from that store,' so it's a win for the store too as well as the wider community."

From a marketing perspective, Stephanie Redcross is all for collaboration between companies that have complementary products. "I'm a little bit hesitant about collaboration between companies with the same type of product. I like to see companies that have adjacent markets, so maybe a shoe company with a sock company because those are things that go together, or a shoe company with a fashion company or a purse company," she says.

"Often, people see these things as individual pieces, but if you look at the way consumers buy, it's usually with the idea of matching an item with something else. So why not, as a business owner, make that match in the beginning? It makes it easier for the consumer and is a win for all the businesses involved," says Redcross.

Nacheez's Ilsa Hess implements this strategy by collaborating with businesses that make complementary vegan products, such as seitan. "I'm currently in talks with a local producer of vegan seitan. We're excited to play with all kinds of yummy recipes using both of our products. I'm happy to share my customers with another vegan company that's making great products my customers will benefit from," says Hess.

Even long-time restaurateurs Joy Pierson and Bart Potenza from Candle Cafe are enhancing their business model through the creation of a frozen food line and a collaboration with another food company.

Other ways to collaborate are to share premises with another vegan business, as Vegan Style does with Las Vegan café; sponsorship—such as Vegan Proteins's sponsorship of athletes who are part of their non-profit organization PlantBuilt, resulting in around 30 vegan athletes directly promoting the company's products; and working with a non-profit organization.

Evolotus PR's Kezia Jauron explains the benefits of teaming up with a non-profit: "While many in the philanthropic community

116

say that the biggest, most effective charities were not hit hard by the economic downturn of 2008 because their programs and services were needed more than ever, there was an impact on smaller, local, and regional charities. So I suggest vegan businesses look for ways to form meaningful partnerships with animal non-profits, such as donating a percentage of profits in a given month to a rescue group or sanctuary, or donating a dollar for every sale of a particular item, whatever is appropriate for your model. That non-profit will help promote your business to their supporters and you'll help promote the non-profit to your customers, so it benefits everyone," says Jauron.

Kevin Newell has increased his business by partnering with an animal welfare charity. "They often get calls in regarding urban wildlife, and our partnership extends to the point where they send all the enquiries to us, as they can't help those contacting them, while we can," he says.

Now, while we have seen that collaboration is a vital and effective strategy to grow your business, that doesn't mean you shouldn't pay attention to your competitors, nor be wary about who you collaborate with.

"You definitely have to be aware of your competition, watch what they're marketing, how they're marketing, what their message is and also be aware of how it's resonating with people. But if you do have direct competition, then that's great; that's a real compliment," says Ella Nemcova. "For one, it shows some faith in what you've created; there's actually a market for it. If there's nothing like your product on the market, it could be that no one has invented it, or it could be that no one wants it. It could be that there isn't a great need for it, so competition is a very good thing to study, just to see what the market requires, what the market demands, how the market flows."

Be mindful to protect your reputation, advises Ron Prasad. "You have to use your own discretion to ascertain whether it's worth doing a joint venture with another business. How well do you know the business owner? Do you trust them? Can they possibly ruin your reputation? Remember, your reputation in business is very important. Do your research on joint ventures, and then make your decision. Sometimes, it will be a no-brainer, and sometimes you will have to think long and hard."

Addiction Food's Georgie Campbell agrees. "A lot of people might be animal rights orientated but it comes down to personally being ethical as well. A lot of the time, people are blinded by a seemingly great business idea, but they have unrealistic expectations or knowledge of what it takes both financially and in work hours to manifest an idea into reality," says Campbell.

Not every collaboration will eventuate, particularly if the company or business isn't run on ethical principles, as Veganpet's Sandy Anderson found out. Anderson is troubled by certain companies jumping on the vegan pet food bandwagon and creating products that simply remove the meat from their existing items, or bringing in so-called vegan cat foods containing no taurine, which is dangerous to the point of potentially killing cats.

"There is no legislation to protect the customer," says Anderson. "And if I start banging a drum about it, it sounds as though I'm just being angry at the competition, and that's not the case at all. They aren't doing it right. They're doing it because they're dollar-driven and they think it's something that they're going to make some money out of. I've approached those companies; I've tried to speak to them about it and say, 'I'll work with you,' but they don't want to hear about it."

Do your research thoroughly on potential collaborators. Find out who the influencers are in your industry and reach out. This can be as simple as connecting and engaging with them on social media, or commenting on their blog. Where possible, meet in person. Remember, everyone is busy, so don't be offended if they decline your invitation. And always figure out what's in it for them. Don't be selfish and immediately ask for something from them—work out what you can offer them that's beneficial to them.

If the person you're looking to collaborate with is a marketing or PR professional or business coach or consultant, don't expect to get free advice. Asking such a professional if you can 'meet for coffee to pick your brain' is insulting, as it implies that their years of study and experience is only worth a few dollars or pounds.

This is how they make their living, so take advantage of any free information they provide on their website, social media platforms, or email lists, but expect to pay to hire them for a consultation. And if you offer these services, consider putting a Rent My Brain section on your website (as I've done for my media coaching). This is a great way to provide consulting services in a one-off or ongoing arrangement. Meeting up with fellow business owners offering similar or complementary products than you is different, although you still need to demonstrate the benefit of them taking time out to meet you.

Networking is essential to spreading the word about your business and finding potential collaborators as well as customers or clients. "As small business owners, I find that we tend to start working in a little bubble because we've got so much to do, but we need to pop it and go out there and talk to people," says Bourgeois Boheme's Alicia Lai. "From my perspective as a retail business, you have to get out there, walk around the shops, and listen to what's going on; sit and watch people to see what shoes they're wearing; and go into creative businesses to see what they're getting up to and getting out of the office."

Victoria Moran also stresses the importance of networking, giving a good example of how a breakfast meeting resulted in media coverage for her daughter's homemade beer. While at breakfast with her literary agent and the agent's two friends, Moran recounted how her daughter Adair and her then fiancé, both aspiring actors, made 'Actor Ale' at home. They included their headshots and acting credentials on the label and gave it to casting directors and agents.

"One of the women at the table happened to be with a very, very large PR firm here in New York City. Within two hours of that breakfast, this PR woman had contacted *The New York Times*, my daughter got a call, and four days later, there was a story three quarters of a page long with two huge pictures about Actor Ale and the life of young actors in the city," explains Moran. "This is PR that most people couldn't afford to pay for on their best day. It happened because I met socially one very influential woman. So vegan business owners may be thinking, 'I can't afford a giant PR firm like that.' But what you have to do is network. You have to get out there and talk to people. I didn't know that this woman was someone with great influence in the world; I was just having breakfast because somebody invited me."

There's a right way and wrong way to network, however. You don't want to be "that" person who rushes around the room pressing a business card into everyone's hand.

Networking tips
Below is a summary of 10 key do's and don'ts in regards to networking:

1. Go with an attitude of giving, not taking. Instead of seeing everyone in the room as a potential client or someone you can use to get money coming into your business, see them as a potential friend, and consider what you can offer them—a helpful tip, a connection that would benefit them, for example.

2. Know why you're attending an event or gathering: Set two or three outcomes you'd like to achieve, such as learning about four people's businesses and stories.

3. Actively listen: Focus on the person you're connecting with and really hear what they're saying. Don't think of what you're going to say next, and don't look around the

room while they're speaking to you.

4. Aim to get others' business cards to take away with you, rather than trying to give yours to all and sundry.

5. Ask open-ended questions about the person and their business: These are questions that can't be answered with a 'yes' or 'no'; they have to be expanded on. Open-ended questions usually start with What, When, Where, How, or Why.

6. Prepare your 'elevator pitch,' which is a brief summary in one sentence explaining who you are, what you do, who you help, and how you help them. Be prepared to adapt your pitch so it doesn't sound rehearsed or stilted.

7. Be confident and friendly: People are attracted to confidence (not arrogance) in another person. Smile.

8. Dress in suitable attire while also retaining your individuality and style. If you're attending a corporate event, turning up in a scruffy t-shirt and ripped jeans probably isn't going to do you or your business any good. Go for smart casual instead. If you love sparkle and bling, like I do, it may not be appropriate to attend a particular event in a sequinned jacket, but you can wear diamante jewelry or cufflinks.

9. Build rapport: Sometimes, this happens naturally or, rather, unconsciously when you "hit it off" with someone immediately after you meet them. Other times, you can employ strategies and techniques to build rapport and connection fast. The quickest way is to find common ground.

10. Follow up: Depending on the level of rapport you felt you built with certain people, follow up with an email or phone call.

Relationship with Adversaries

By adversaries, I mean people who work in animal abuse industries, and I use the term *adversary* as something likely to be traditionally perceived as such, rather than an actual enemy.

As I said in the Introduction, and as many of the vegan business owners interviewed for this book have said, running a vegan business is a form of activism. As vegan business owners who are often also animal advocates, we're exposed to atrocities that trouble, distress, and traumatize us. It's essential to communicate calmly and professionally, including online. Take a stand, by all means, but it doesn't help your business to name-call or be seen to be aggressive.

Bed and Broccoli's Nikki Medwell takes the approach of befriending her neighbors, most of whom perpetuate animal abuse through their dairy businesses.

"When we first moved here, we didn't think too much about the fact that it was a dairy food bowl; we just thought, 'This is the right property for us.' We went ahead, bought it, and started to renovate. Then we thought, 'What are the neighbors going to think? Bloody vegans have moved in!' But, through hindsight, we learned that they felt equally threatened, thinking, 'What's going on? Why are these people here? Are they here to photograph us? Are they here to break into our dairies in the night?'

"So they were threatened by us, and we were thinking that it's such a small community, and we're going to get run out of town. It's through being great friends with our neighbors, who are the biggest dairy farmers in the district and know everybody else, that they've been able to quash the fears of most of the other farmers. They said, 'Hey, Scott and Nikki are actually really nice people; we've been to their house for dinner, and the food is lovely,'" says Medwell.

This approach has even resulted in the dairy farmers promoting Bed and Broccoli. "One of them had to go overseas to Dubai for a water-saving conference that the government had organized and he was telling me how they had dinner, during which he told his colleagues that he lives next to Australia's first vegan bed and breakfast," Medwell chuckles. "And it's because we don't judge them and we treat them as equals that we get these benefits. They know we don't agree with what they do, and we just leave it at that, and if they ask questions, we answer. But apart from that, they're human beings, and they just haven't made that connection yet. Just because these people haven't got there yet, it doesn't mean that they're nasty, horrible, and we want to ostracize them. They're actually our target market. Hanging out with vegans all the time is preaching to the choir, so now we look back and think this is the most perfect decision we could've made, putting ourselves right here, in the middle of a dairy food bowl!" says Medwell.

Chapter 5
Branding

The major challenge cited by the vegan business owners interviewed for this book is marketing—how to attract new customers as well as encourage existing ones to keep buying from you. Before we go on to marketing in the next few chapters, it's important to establish your brand, as the two work hand in hand.

Sydney-based branding consultant Sara Kidd explains the difference between the two: "Branding is the process of creating the entire look, feel, name, language, and behaviors related to your business, product, or person. It's different than marketing, as your brand is what represents your business, product, or person. Marketing is the tool you use to expose your brand to your targeted demographic," says Kidd.

In his book, *Unconscious Branding,* author Douglas Van Praet reveals what most marketers have ignored over the years: that we don't buy based on logic, but on emotion, which we then justify with logic. For example, you buy a pair of shoes because you're excited about how you're going to look wearing them. Then you tell yourself how you needed them for work. We buy based on subconscious behaviors that we're generally unaware of, making most market research surveys unreliable. Van Praet found the reasons focus groups give for choosing a particular brand are different from the actual reasons for their choice.

The more a brand can inspire emotion, the more likely we are to engage with it. This is why companies are getting into "native advertising" on large media sites. Native advertising is content in the form of editorial. It tells a story. It could be a moving or inspiring video clip telling the story of a person or animal. It just happens to be created by a brand, instead of by a media outlet. The idea is that the positive feelings the consumer experiences when taking in the content get associated with the brand. It's a far cry from traditional advertising, which comes from a "Buy this because it's great" approach.

We touched on market research in Chapter 3, and we'll look at it again in the next chapter on marketing, but one of the reasons it's so important is because your brand must reflect the values of your audience. For example, if you're going to charge more for organic products or place yourself at the luxury end of a market, your brand must reflect this.

"Establishing a strong consistent brand is important, as it tells your targeted audience who you are, what you offer, and how you fit into the marketplace. It also creates credibility, trust, and a foundation for your business to expand and grow," says Kidd.

The Regal Vegan's Ella Nemcova has implemented this strategy and advises others to establish their brand voice early on. "Play a long game. Be clear as to what kind of business you're building. Establish what your brand voice is early on and never stray from it. If you're a high-end brand, you don't suddenly become cheap. You don't suddenly do coupons in the newspaper, you stay a high-end brand. You associate with high-end events and high-end stores," says Nemcova.

This applies to the words you use, which also reflect your brand. Fans of entrepreneur Marie Forleo enjoy her sassy expressions, which are backed up with smart, insightful business and lifestyle advice. She can get away with spouting the "Jersey girl" lingo because it's an authentic part of her brand.

"It's important to learn how to build your brand architecture and what words always reflect your brand," says Nemcova. "When people say, 'I'm looking for decadent vegan food or fancy vegan appetizers,' The Regal Vegan is going to come to their mind. We always portray the product that way. When our product is shot, it's not shot ever looking like hummus."

The Cruelty Free Shop's Jessica Bailey also learned the value of not cheapening her brand. "There's nothing we can do to compete with big supermarkets or the mainstream products, and trying to is pointless; all that does is cheapen your brand and put you out of business," she says. "We've come to the conclusion that we have to sell products at a certain price point to stay in business, so we price our products at that level. Yes, we're more expensive than the mainstream, but people understand that and are prepared to pay a bit more, not just for the product itself but also for the service that comes with it."

Branding Mistakes
According to Kidd, business owners generally make the following mistakes with their branding:
1. The owner creates a brand that they like without considering the demographic they want to target. Just because you like it, doesn't mean everyone else will.
2. You decide to do the branding and design yourself because you don't want to pay a professional.
3. The branding for the company is well targeted but the personal branding of the owners/executives is not. You're a direct reflection of your business.
4. A lack of understanding about what your demographic wants (not needs) and failing to give it to them.

To avoid these pitfalls, Kidd advises working with professionals who understand branding, design, and the behaviors of your demographic and who can work on your personal branding.

"How do you want to represent your business and how do you want your audience to see you? Personal branding will increase the value of your business. If your demographic likes you, they'll want to buy you and everything you offer. Working on yourself is just as important as working on your business," says Kidd.

126

Invest in Branding from the Start

Ms. Cupcake's Mellissa Morgan stresses the importance of investing in your branding from the get-go.

"You need to know everything about your brand because once you know what your brand is, you will understand the voice your brand speaks in. It will also dictate who your customers are going to be. For example, we don't do high-end weddings. That's not something we specialize in and you wouldn't really come to a crazy cupcake-hat-wearing lady to do your elegant, traditional wedding. But if you're looking for an over-the-top, fun, indulgent cake for a child who has a serious egg allergy, you're going to come to our business," says Morgan, who advocates for all new business owners to invest half of whatever money they have up front on branding.

"If you've got $4,000, you spend $2,000 on branding; if you've got £400, you spend £200 on branding. We all see these Facebook pages that have homemade logos on them and while we know that you're doing the best you can, as a consumer, I'm not going to have confidence that you're going to be able to produce a product as good as someone else who has a very professional-looking logo on their website. So even if it means going to a graphic design student, do whatever you can to get your branding done by a professional right at the beginning because it will pay off for years to come," says Morgan.

Personal Brand vs. Business Brand

If you're following the thought leader model in which you are your brand, your personal branding must be integrated into your business branding. However, even if your business isn't based around you, you're still the face of the business, so you need to ensure that your personal brand doesn't contradict your business brand.

This applies to whoever is the face of your brand. If you're in a position to hire celebrities to endorse your brand, make sure they're aligned with your values. This is why large corporations drop public figures if they do something that doesn't fit with the values of the brand. Choose your ambassadors carefully.

Vegan Mainstream's Stephanie Redcross warns that your personal brand can distract from your business brand. "Sometimes people can get their personal passion and perspective on life mixed up with their business's image. Speaking personally, there are things that may have nothing to do with Vegan Mainstream that I enjoy doing," says Redcross. "I have to be careful what I put out there about my personal life to ensure it doesn't detract from my business's brand and connect Vegan Mainstream with ideology that isn't related to our mission statement. This doesn't mean you shouldn't show your personal side; it's more of an exercise in sharing information that's relevant to the brand experience."

That said, authenticity is crucial to your branding. Unconsciously, we can all smell BS. We know instinctively when someone is being fake or putting on an act or trying to be someone they're not.

Tofurky's Seth Tibbott found this out to his cost while running his tempeh business in the early days. Despite living in a tree house, he tried to appear conservative. "I'm a fun-loving person, and before Tofurky, I tried to be something I wasn't. I tried to be this straight-looking businessman because I thought that's what you're supposed to look like," says Tibbott.

This meant that the company had little humor in its marketing. But as soon as Tibbott embraced his colorful and fun-loving personality, it rubbed off into the promotion of Tofurky.

"People drew pictures of what a Tofurky would look like in the wild and we got on board with that and had fun with it. Before that, I really hadn't tried to have fun. I like to have fun; that's just who I am. It was an authentic move, so Tofurky was an extension of this fun-loving streak of mine, and it happened to work out because others had fun with the brand."

At the other end of the scale, Lee Coates of Ethical Investors and Cruelty Free Super has created a personal brand around being "Mr Establishment." "I've been in financial services for 34 years. That's all I've done, and I've taken as many exams as possible to be qualified. I'm one of the top 150 accredited financial planners out of 30,000 in the UK, so I'm at the top of my area of specialty. I've been awarded an OBE [Order of the British Empire] medal for services to ethical businesses in finance. I'm so ultra-establishment that when I start talking about something different, such as ethical money and investing in a cruelty-free superannuation fund, it's not coming from the weird and wacky, it's coming from the center," says Coates.

Branding to Stand Out from the Crowd

As we'll see in the next chapter on marketing, it's essential to have a unique selling proposition (USP), which is something that makes you or your product or service stand out from the rest.

"By really understanding your audience, and knowing the right audience to target, you have the opportunity to create a strong and stable brand that will directly resonate with them," says Sara Kidd. "They will want to buy your product or service because it 'feels' right. Everything about your brand aligns with their values and behaviors, making the purchase an easy decision. The colors, fonts, textures, ingredients, and technologies all matter when creating a strong brand. A brand creates trust between you and your customer, securing return business."

This trust can serve a business well, particularly during slow periods or even an economic downturn. "Continue to be consistent with your branding behaviors as much as possible," advises Kidd. "If your business is known for releasing a weekly newsletter, having fast response times, or really positive messaging, stick to those behaviors. People respond well to brands they know they can rely on."

Standing out from the crowd not only can make you memorable

to clients, it can also land you media opportunities or publishing deals, as was the case with Ms. Cupcake's Mellissa Morgan. "Publishers see that you've got this direct audience who like your product and your brand, so chances are some of them are going to buy your book. But if you only have 100 followers on Facebook and you approach a publisher to say you want to write a cookbook, they're not really going to listen, regardless of how great your recipes are. So you do often need to build your brand and then the other things will follow," says Morgan.

'No Compromise' Branding

For some vegan-run businesses, their 'no compromise' attitude is part of their brand. "No compromise is my message," says image consultant Ginger Burr. "I stand firmly in my commitment to cruelty-free fashion and creating awareness and change with people who are willing. In the nearly 10 years since I became vegan, the availability and visibility of vegan fashion choices has grown exponentially. I know that will continue, and I'll be at the forefront of that growth." Burr's stance has already yielded success on the PR front. *VegNews* magazine chose her as one of the "25 Most Fascinating Vegetarians" in 2007 for her "groundbreaking" work as a vegan image consultant.

Candle Cafe's Joy Pierson and Bart Potenza realized the importance of not compromising on their principles, when they considered using organic milk and eggs shortly after they moved to their new location in the early days when business was quiet. Pierson recounts a phone conversation she had with an "organic" milk farmer, in which he stated that the process of extracting milk involved "raping" the cows to impregnate them and removing their babies who are slaughtered for veal after just one day.

"I was shocked at his honesty," Pierson admits. "I said to him, 'But you're an organic farmer; why only a day?' And he said, 'Lady, either *you* want the milk or you want the baby cow to have the milk.' And I said, 'I'm very clear—I want the baby to have the milk.'" So that really confirmed our decision not to compromise on our vegan ethics."

Jivamukti Yoga's Sharon Gannon had a similar experience when a high-profile fashion designer gave her 1,000 pieces of her white cotton yoga clothing line to sell in the Jivamukti shop. But because it wasn't organic, Gannon declined the gift.

"I told her, 'I really want this boutique to only carry organic or recycled material, and if I don't do it, then nobody will. I have to set the standard.' And the designer said, 'You're crazy!' I realized it might be a bad business move, but this is my life. I'm going to try to do something with it that enhances the world. So I said, 'No, thank you' to her gift, and, of course, a year later she came out with her organic line!" says Gannon, laughing.

Ethics Informs Branding

One of the reasons Gannon started the Jivamukti Yoga School, which runs on ethical vegan principles including truthfulness and non-harming, was because of her experience at a health center she taught at that cheated its clientele.

"One time, I came to teach and there was a sign on the door that said, 'We're sorry everybody, we're closed.' They couldn't pay their bills so they decided to close down, but they had sold memberships right up to the day they closed and didn't even tell the staff. We were left out in the cold," says Gannon. "After that experience, I said to myself, 'If I'm ever in that kind of position as an owner of a business that has employees who are dependent, I'll never do that.' So my partner David Life and I worked really hard to make sure that we always have reserve money in case a catastrophe happens so we could take care of our employees and not do anything so dishonest as to cheat people."

Advocates of traditional business models may perceive these types of principled stands as "bad" for business, but it's increasingly the case that consumers aren't simply buying a product, they're buying a brand and what it stands for.

"More people are not only looking to see about the ethical stance of the product itself but also the ethical stance of the company," says Plamil Foods's Adrian Ling. "And if that company is producing dairy products or non-vegan products, more consumers are asking themselves, 'Why should I give this company my money?' Even though it's being spent on a vegan product, why should it create profit for a company that is also producing non-vegan items?"

Ayana Organics's Samantha Crosby agrees. "I believe knowing that Ayana is a vegan-owned and operated company, rather than a company that sells vegan products alongside other non-vegan products, makes a difference in terms of trust and reliability, and it helps us to stand out among hundreds of other businesses," says Crosby.

Lee Coates is another example of how a company's ethics can result in more clients and greater profits. In Coates's case, his Ethical Investors business gives away 50 percent of its profits to charities and organizations that benefit people, animals, and the planet—a move that was unheard of in the financial planning sector. "It generates more new customers and more business for us because we're seen to be more conscious and more ethical in the way we do business, and if it's us versus another ethical adviser, most people will say, 'I chose you because you give half your profits away,'" says Coates.

Personalized Service Branding

We saw in Chapter 4 that outstanding customer service is key to standing out as a brand and retaining a regular and loyal clientele of raving fans who can't wait to tell all and sundry about how fabulous your product, service, or business is.

Factoring in a "wow" experience for your customer (remember, people buy based on how you or your product or service makes them feel) is a smart way to build your brand.

Giacomo Marchese and Dani Taylor, the team behind Vegan

Proteins, are known for sending a hand-written and decorated box to each customer. While many other brands do bulk shipping in the same bland, homogenized cartons, Vegan Proteins offers a personalized service which results in the brand standing out from the rest, including much larger brands. They are "zigging" when everyone else is "zagging."

"We're all about being friendly and putting more of a human personality into our customer service, and people see that and go, 'Wow, this business actually cares about me,'" says Marchese. "We know that we're nowhere near being able to compete with huge brands such as Amazon, so we don't try," adds Taylor. "We aim to make a real connection with as many of our customers as possible, and let them know how valued they are. People love getting their boxes with little doodles on them. As we grew, we were afraid we wouldn't be able to keep up with all of the orders being so individualized, but we decided it was so important to who we are as a brand that we were going to keep doing it no matter how big we got. So we now have an office worker whose sole responsibility is to decorate boxes and write 'thank you' notes."

And as we saw from Chapter 4, Veganpet's Sandy Anderson's commitment to quality and customer service is what makes her brand stand out from larger companies and attract loyal customers who will pay more for these elements.

Approachable and Lifestyle Branding

Approachability is what the GUNAS brand is about, says owner Sugandh G. Agrawal. "I want people to feel that I'm approachable, my brand is approachable, my products are approachable. The people who are my target audience want that approachability, whether it's with the product or with the designer. So, I think that's what really helps me stand out as a brand," says Agrawal.

For Nichole Dandrea, positioning Nicobella as a lifestyle brand rather than putting a focus on chocolate-making was important. "My personal passion is plant-based eating, but it's also giving back to the animal community, so it's really ethically driven as well. It's around compassion, healthy eating, and taking care of the environment. So it's more of a lifestyle company, and I'm trying to focus more on the lifestyle rather than focusing on having everything be all about chocolate. I just let chocolate be the vehicle to get the messages across," says Dandrea.

Health as Branding

Iku Wholefood started in Sydney, Australia in 1985. Current owner, Ken Israel, took it over in 1990. From the start, it was centered around healthy eating.

"When Iku started, it followed the Japanese macrobiotic discipline. With the name Iku, the emphasis was on being Zen and clean-cut; always use natural, always use timber, but we were very conscious of not looking too brown-colored in terms of our décor, or too organic, or too herbal, so it had quite a slick look, which I brought to the business," explains Israel.

"Now, the natural trend in food and architecture has hit, everything is rough-sawn, natural-cut timber; even butcher shops and banks are now using this. It's like everybody wants something natural but most places offer the same thing and nobody goes to the extent that we do."

Iku is renowned for not microwaving its meals and using organic ingredients whenever possible. It's this focus on healthy wholefoods, which happen to be all plant-based, that has kept a loyal clientele going through the doors of its central location in Glebe as well as franchises in other Sydney suburbs. This brand awareness and reputation has resulted in Israel discussing opportunities to supply Iku-branded food in other retail outlets.

222 Veggie Vegan's Ben Asamani also centers his brand around promoting healthy wholefood, again with no microwaving.

"I don't cook anything that's hard, such as hard rice or pasta so that makes us different from some other restaurants," says Asamani. "I believe in whole food, nothing refined. We also don't deep fry anything here. I believe in baking. You see the difference between something that's fried and something that's baked, but most restaurants don't worry about it. Many restaurants, including vegetarian ones, use microwave ovens to heat the food, but it kills the food. When customers learn this, it makes a difference for them and they support us."

Educating people about healthy eating has played a key role in Asamani's business journey. "Sometimes people ask me, 'Why don't you use vinegar?' And I explain why I only use apple cider vinegar because most others aren't good for you. I also make sure any soya we use is organic and if someone comes in and says they're on a special diet or allergic to peanuts, I listen and create something especially for them. This makes a huge difference for customers," says Asamani.

And as we saw from Chapter 4, Asamani's customers love the 222 brand and its commitment to their well-being so much that they purposefully frequent it to ensure it stays open.

Visual Branding

Some brands are recognizable because of their strong visual element. As we saw earlier with Ms. Cupcake, the brand is all about color, eccentricity, fun, indulgence, and decadence, which makes it memorable.

Vx, a one-stop vegan boutique in London's Kings Cross, sells a diverse range of products, from "vegan junk food" and shoes to a unique collection of rare and unusual items, and an exclusive range of Secret Society of Vegans (SSOV) products, including fashion wear. "Vx and SSOV have a strong visual personality or personality in general," says owner Rudy Penando. "We stand out naturally."

Innovation as Branding

Also committed to creating innovative as well as eco-friendly and vegan couture is Canadian brand ESPE.

"Every season, we rigorously deliver new and innovative designs," says owner Eva Fung. "We believe that, in the long run, customers will appreciate the quality and creativity behind our brand. Innovative and style-savvy designs as well as the use of vibrant palettes are something that the vegan market is craving and yet lacking. Perfecting them helps to boost our brand and set us apart from our competition. Vegan doesn't necessarily mean bland."

This approach of innovation and creativity has already given ESPE a strong competitive edge and led to it becoming a sought-after brand. "A lot of handbag and wallet companies are still using leather for their products. We've set our own standards, and we've committed to not using leather while keeping the quality and durability of our products. The fact that we have over 90 percent new designs every season sets us apart from our competition," says Fung. "We also experiment with different manufacturing processes, such as embossing, imprinting, stitching, and so on, to create outstanding effects on our products. The key is to get customers excited with our newness every season."

Rebranding

Because of the time, effort, and money that goes into creating a brand, it's best to get it right from the start. However, if, as you go forward, you realize you made a mistake and are unhappy with your branding, don't be afraid to rebrand.

Bourgeois Boheme's Alicia Lai did just this. After taking a break of two years, Lai returned with a completely different positioning, rebranding from the lower end of the shoe market to become a luxury, aspirational brand.

"Previously, we stocked other brands and were a lower price point, but it really wasn't what I wanted to do," says Lai, who stresses that Bourgeois Boheme isn't just about shoes but about lifestyle. "It's not necessarily product, product, product. It's about looking at a brand, at the lifestyle and the content behind it as well. Yes, we do want to sell shoes, but, at the same time, it's about getting people to think you're an aspirational brand. We have this concept and lifestyle around what we're doing and we're bringing this to the mainstream as well as the vegan market," says Lai.

How to Hire a Branding Consultant

You may be clear on aspects of your brand, but as Sara Kidd noted earlier, it's wise to hire a professional who understands the different elements required to form a consistent, targeted brand identity that will appeal to and attract your desired clientele.

Kidd offers the following advice on how to go about hiring a branding expert: "Always get recommendations from people you trust who have already worked with them. Ask for examples from the professional and shop around. Make sure the person you're hiring is vegan or at least understands your vegan values. This really helps. Meet with them in person if you can or via Skype and discuss what you're wanting to achieve. Get a feel for them and make sure they're someone you want to work with. Also, when working with graphic designers, remember that they don't always have a background in branding. Usually their main goal is to design something you're happy with, not what your audience wants," says Kidd.

Becoming laser clear on your market is essential, adds Kidd. "Are you wanting to market to the mainstream or to people who have already converted to veganism? Can you compete in these markets? What is the end goal for your business or product? Is your business international or local? There are many different variables to look at in this situation. Hiring a branding consultant is a great way to work through these questions and make sure that your branding and its entire look, feel, name, language, and behaviors resonate with your customers or clients."

Chapter 6
Marketing

If *selling* is a dirty word for some vegan business owners, so too is *marketing*. It's often seen as narcissistic, self-promoting, pushy, and vain. Sometimes, marketing *can* be unethical, using manipulative techniques to trick people into buying something they don't want or need. If you've ever attended a seminar, been whipped up into an emotional frenzy, herded to the back of the room in a trance and spent hundreds or thousands of dollars on a product or service that didn't deliver what it promised, you likely fell victim to unethical marketing practices.

Internet marketing, in particular, has got a bad rap, with the worst offenders smashing people's trust and making it harder for ethical marketers in that space to cut through. We're currently in an era where terms such as *conscious* or *heart-centered* marketing are being bandied around. While the intentions behind their use may be good and the users are attempting to distance themselves from traditional marketers, I find the terms pretentious and a bit too desperate, begging consumers to trust them. And if marketers are using those terms while promoting animal-based products, the terms are also incongruous.

Authentic marketing is the buzzword of the moment and, when done well, is more likely to resonate with your target market. It's about being transparent and true to your values. No more contrived strategies designed to force a sale. No more brands trying to be something they're not. Artificiality is out and "realness" is in. Honesty and transparency are key.

"A lot of marketing that's thrown at customers today is very pretentious," asserts GUNAS's Sugandh G. Agrawal. "They're trying to portray an image of someone that people want to be rather than who they are, and I feel that, with GUNAS, what I've done is try to portray an image of the person as they really are, what they really want to be, what they really want to stand for, and what they want to show with the power of their purchase through the products they buy."

People are looking for honesty in the products they buy nowadays and are tired of being duped and lied to, adds Agrawal. "There's no pretense here. In fact, I encourage people to ask me as many questions as they have about the brand or the processes, the materials, and I'm always honest about it. I'm not perfect; I don't have the perfect solution to everything, but I'm on a path of constantly discovering that perfection. I feel that my customers appreciate that honesty, and they like the marriage between that honesty and high fashion because people don't usually associate the two together."

Nicobella's Nichole Dandrea has also found that being real and genuine with customers through her marketing brings about more engagement with her brand and more sales than marketing strategies that are based on the "hard sell" approach.

"Previously, I'd send out a newsletter about the products and promote it on social media and we didn't get a response. We have a lot of chocolate and we have to get a sale, but I found that if I take a step back, go to yoga practice, meditate a while, and get back in touch with the real reason why I'm doing this business and then write something about that, it gets people's attention much more," says Dandrea. "It could be a post about meditation or passion or healthy eating—something a bit more meaningful that has quality content that came from the heart. When you're relating to people and having a conversation with them, it's a lot more effective than just trying to throw a sale at them."

Earlier in this book, we looked at reframing, whereby we take a concept, experience, or belief and change the way we perceive it. So, if the thought of marketing fills you with dread, think of it as psychologist Clare Mann pointed out in Chapter 2: Sharing your product or service with people who are eagerly seeking your solution to their problems. It's not about convincing someone to buy something they neither want nor need.

The Importance of Marketing

Before we look at different ways to market your products or services, I want you to really understand why you can't afford to ignore marketing or dismiss it.

Author, consultant, and vegan lifestyle coach JL Fields believes you must advocate for yourself and your business. "When I was executive director for non-profit organizations, I was my advocate, and it's no different when you're running a small business. You just have to consider the public as your board of directors. You have to tell them how awesome you are because there's no other way that they're going to know it. So, you have to get rid of this idea that being humble is wonderful," says Fields. "Being humble is good, but it doesn't mean that you also don't tell people how great you are. You have to find that place where you can tell your narrative of what you're capable of doing."

Evolotus PR's Kezia Jauron puts it more bluntly. "If you're not going to market your business, then you're just not serious enough about your business, and you might want to go back to working for The Man," she says.

Jauron is right. You can have the best products or services in the world, but if no one knows about them, you have a hobby, not a business. And here's another reframe: If you've gone to the trouble of creating fantastic products and services that are good for people, animals, and the planet and you don't let people know about them, you're doing a disservice to the world.

You're doing a disservice to potential customers by depriving them of your creations, you're doing yourself a disservice by sabotaging your gift and your business, and you're doing animals a disservice by not enabling people to buy an ethical product or service. If you consider your vegan business as a form of activism, you must get your head around marketing and selling. Because activism is all about selling—it's about selling a concept that animals are not ours to use, abuse, exploit, or kill—and your vegan product or service is the solution.

Think about the creative arts: singers, musicians, visual artists, actors, performers, dancers. The ones who attain international fame aren't necessarily the best in their field, but they do have the best marketing. There are countless unheralded talents with remarkable gifts who no one has heard of because they know how to create but not how to market.

"On some level, those of us who create for a living think we're frauds," says The Regal Vegan's Ella Nemcova. "We think we're faking it because we made it up, forgetting that's us being creative and actually making stuff up is what gives us the capacity to become business owners, to become inventors, to become brands, to become products, to become entrepreneurs. It's that courage to get out there and put something into the world that didn't exist before."

Market to the Right People
In Chapter 3, we touched on the importance of market research—ensuring that your product or service is a valid one that people want or need and will buy. Key to this is drilling down and becoming clear on who your target audience is.

As vegan business owners, it's easy to say, "everyone" when asked who our target market is, but when you market to everyone, you end up marketing to no one. This "spray and pray" approach may have worked with the traditional "build it and they will come" business models. But that's no longer the case. Technology has changed the way we consume information. Blogs, online magazines, digital tablet magazines, podcasts, apps, video streaming sites, and social media have led to an explosion in the numbers of outlets creating and curating specialized content for targeted audiences.

You must be so clear on your ideal customer: where they live (down to the suburb), what kind of job they have, how much they earn, and more, so that your marketing speaks directly to them and they believe that you understand them.

"What you're doing is creating ease and finding solutions for people for the problems in their lives. So if you've found the right target, you really are solving a problem. They'll welcome you," says Ella Nemcova. "They'll welcome you because they've been looking for what you have to offer. If I told you that what I have for you is going to solve a lot of your problems and create a lot of joy for you and give you more time, would you want to listen?"

One of the mistakes business owners make is to focus their marketing on their product or service, rather than on the potential buyer. Speaker and executive coach Ron Prasad provides a good example:

"I've asked one simple question to many small business owners: 'Why should I buy from you?' The stock standard answer that I get nine times out of 10 is along the lines of, 'Because I'm one of the best in this industry' or, 'Because my products are of the best quality' or, 'Because I'll deliver a service that no one else will deliver,'" explains Prasad. "Did you notice that one key word is missing from all those statements? That key word is *you*. What about *you* the buyer?"

Contrast that with the following example of a human resources manager asking Prasad the question: "Why should I hire you to provide communications training for my staff?"

"My response will be along the lines of, 'When you invest in communications training, your staff will walk away with absolute clarity on how to communicate assertively, how to communicate diplomatically in conflict resolution, how to engage in effective listening, and how to write with professionalism, integrity, and empathy. You do want accelerated professional development for your staff, and are committed to their excellence, aren't you?'

"Do you see the words *I, me* or *my* in that response? And, I have finished my response with a question. That means the ball is in their court now, and it's their turn to talk. Simple strategies like this can make a massive difference," says Prasad.

When putting together a marketing strategy or copy, keep in mind the three-step rule:
1. State a problem that your buyer might have.
2. Offer them a solution (your product or service).
3. Give them a call to action (buy your product or service—and be clear about how they can do this).

The better you understand your potential and existing customers' wants and needs, the more you can communicate to them in their language, using words and phrases that resonate with them, the more they'll feel you understand them, and the more aligned they'll become to your brand and trust you to deliver.

Download a free customer profile questionnaire from Vegan Business Media: **www.veganbusinessmedia.com/customerprofile**

What is Your Unique Selling Proposition (USP)?

As we saw in the previous chapter on branding, a USP in marketing lingo is something that's special and particular to your brand, product, or service. It's that something extra that makes you stand out from the rest—and that now includes other vegan businesses.

"Business owners need to state what is unique about their product, besides being vegan," says Vegan Mainstream's Stephanie Redcross. "Ten years ago, you were *the* vegan cheese, you were *the* vegan mayo, you were *the* vegan X. Now that's starting to change and evolve. There's more competition in the vegan market. If your business or product is going to survive, you need to be able to say what other benefits you bring and why someone should buy your product."

Educating potential customers is essential, adds Redcross. "It's easy to assume that people will understand the passion you have as a business owner. You might suppose that customers know what it takes to do what you do, and that they get the differences between what you're offering and what else is out there in the market. I'm not saying to go head to head with other companies and start talking badly about your competitors in the market—that's never advisable. But it's important to actually state some of the differences between your product and others."

In the case of Tofurky, its USP is fun. "It was such a crazy product—a lot of people didn't think that anybody would be silly enough to market it," laughs founder Seth Tibbott. "They didn't think there was a market, but here were all these vegetarians and vegans who were left out of the Christmas and Thanksgiving dinner parties because they had to eat salad and potatoes. I love salad and I love potatoes, but nobody had created a high-protein substitute for turkey that sat in the middle of your table as part of the grand feast."

This uniqueness and being first to market resulted in prolific media coverage for Tofurky, catapulting its success. And as we saw in the previous chapter on branding, fun is part of the brand and marketing strategy, including holding competitions asking what a Tofurky looks like in the wild. "We like to take ourselves not too seriously and have some fun, and our marketing truly reflects that," says Tibbott.

You're not limited to just one USP. In Tofurky's case other USPs are that the company is one of the few family-held and independent businesses that has not sold out to larger corporations. It also avoids heavily processed and industrialized soy ingredients, favoring instead organic soy.

For food and catering businesses, a diverse menu, signature dishes, style of delivery, sustainability measures, or health benefits can be your USP. The Veggie Grill chain's standout is providing a broad menu of healthy meals in a fast, casual environment. Candle 79 is at the other end of the spectrum, offering patrons a high-end, organic, fine-dining experience.

The point of difference for Titbits Catering, a vegan catering company in the UK's Brighton, is a weekly changing menu with a different global theme to keep customers interested, in addition to loyalty cards offering a free starter or dessert after five visits.

Bounty Burgers's Loren Lembke promotes the health aspects combined with taste and convenience to position the burgers as a cut above the rest. "They're precooked so you're saving on your electricity bill straight away, they cook up from frozen in several minutes or you can pop them in the toaster. They're very low in fat, have as much protein as meat, high in fiber, with low salt, low carbs, zero cholesterol, and just 95 calories. They also taste delicious," says Lembke.

Australian brand Funky Pies offers vegan versions of the traditional "pie 'n mash" feast with peas and gravy at its shop in Sydney's Bondi Beach. The company's commitment to people, animals and planet has seen it be recognized and frequented regularly by the local community, as well as vegan consumers. "All our staff uniforms are made in sweatshop-free factories, we use biodegradable packaging in all our takeaway products, and our coffee is organic and fair trade," says owner Angie Stephenson.

For fashion brands and online shopping sites, creating and selling innovative products is the key to success. "I try to keep the inventory fresh and new with unique items that you can't find on our competitors' sites," says Ecolissa's Melissa Dion.

Bourgeois Boheme's Alicia Lai stands apart from the majority of vegan shoe brands through classic designs with luxurious finishes. "A lot of vegan shoe companies offer simple designs that are quite similar to each other's offerings. So, there's a lot of repetition. We wanted to be different. Our designs are unique to us and are priced in the luxury range to appeal to that market," says Lai.

ESPE founder Eva Fung takes a similar approach, which, as we saw in the previous chapter on branding, gives her company a competitive edge. Fung is a firm believer in being unique and setting your own trends and standards, rather than following others. "If your products are too similar to others in the market, maybe it's time to try something new. If you have an amazing, differentiable product, people will notice you," says Fung.

People are drawn, particularly to ethical brands, because of what you stand for. So, it's important to market your USPs. In the case of Ethical Wares, a long-running online vegan shoeware company in the UK, letting website visitors know that the owners, Mike Newman and his wife Denise, look after more than 50 rescued animals attracts loyal customers.

"Make sure you include in your marketing that you're passionate about people, animals, and the planet," says Mike Newman. "You have to do all you can do to keep people interested in what you're doing, always looking at bringing in new lines, and keeping people up to date with everything you're doing, without being too pushy. There is a much bigger vegan marketplace available now than when we first started. One of our longest-standing customers used to go hiking in bare feet before he could get vegan walking boots from us. Not too many vegan shoe companies have been around as long as us though. We communicate our commitment to fair trade, for a Free Tibet, and to our own rescued animals through our marketing, and let compassionate people decide if they want to shop with us."

Plamil Foods's Adrian Ling points out the marketing advantage of producing and offering vegan-only products. "For someone who's starting a vegan business, this is a particularly important point because it can be one of their strengths, as this is going to be an issue that grows and grows," he says.

Making these values clear in your marketing also helps explain to potential customers why your product may be priced in the premium range. "When customers commented on the prices of some of the products in my shop, I would talk to them about what the products were made of, how they were made, and the fact that they were made using fair labor practices," says Cow Jones Industrials's Donna Oakes-Jones.

Living your message and being "on brand" is part of an authentic marketing strategy. Mary Prenon's USP for her vegan day spa Le Petite Spa in New York is her own skin. She literally is her message.

"I'm 57 years old and people can't believe it when I tell them. Of course, I don't look 20, but people usually tell me I look like I'm in my early 40s, which I'm totally fine with!" says Prenon, laughing. "I tell them that I've been using the certified organic and vegan Yum Gourmet skincare line from Canada for the past five years, and this is how the products will make your skin look. I also tell them that with these products, they use only a small portion and that they'll actually last much longer than other non-organic, non-vegan products, making them more affordable and sustainable."

Being noticed often requires you to do the opposite of what everyone else in your industry is doing. Sometimes, it's risky, particularly if business is slow or you're in the middle of an economic downturn, but, as Einstein is quoted as saying, "The definition of insanity is doing the same thing over and over again and expecting a different result."

"Any business should be prepared for a downturn. No one knows when it will come. When business slows down, you have to ask yourself, 'What can I do differently than my competitors?'" says Ron Prasad, who recalls a strategy employed by luxury car brand Lexus. "During an economic downturn, a Lexus dealership was sending salesmen to events and functions where people in the high-income bracket attended. The salesmen offered the high-income earners the key to a Lexus for a test drive, without any obligation. Sales picked up, and the economic downturn wasn't felt by this dealership. In this case, the salesmen went to the customers, instead of waiting for the customers to come to them. When business slows down, you have to think outside the square, and do things that customers wouldn't expect. Your point of difference can be your biggest asset," says Prasad.

Market to More Than One Group of People

We noted earlier that defining a particular group of people to market to is important. But it doesn't mean you're restricted to only one demographic; it simply means that, if your product or service has a broad appeal, you market it differently to each particular segment of the population.

For example, if you offer live or online vegan cooking classes, your marketing to busy young mothers would be different to your marketing aimed at men aged 50 and above. The imagery, words, phrases, and style would be different, even though your offering is primarily the same.

Some vegan businesses start out with vegans as their main market and then broaden into non-vegans, while some kick off immediately targeting non-vegans. Since the latter are far more numerous and who we want to reach with our vegan vision, it makes sense to focus our marketing efforts on them.

"When business owners create vegan products they often think 'vegan product equals vegan customer,' but in reality that's not the equation," says Stephanie Redcross. "Truthfully, the people who are going to keep most businesses alive are non-vegans. Maybe their cousin is vegan, or they might have a daughter who's vegan and that's how they initially got introduced to the product. But they continue to buy it because they love the taste, or because it's local, or because it's fair trade. They continue to buy it because of a whole range of other reasons that people have when making choices. And I think a lot of business owners forget to consider that and work it into their marketing."

PlantBased Solutions's David Benzaquen agrees and stresses the important role marketing plays in changing people's perceptions of vegan products as being more expensive by being relatable to many communities who don't traditionally feel welcomed to our table.

"It's important to ensure that the products, images, and words being used are relatable to the millions of people who share our common values of safer and more sustainable communities, healthier food for this and future generations, and a world in which good food is a right, rather than a privilege. One key consideration is how to use effective market research to determine what would sway non-vegan audiences to purchase or consume your product. In doing this, you can ensure that your branding and messaging appeals and relates to these audiences," says Benzaquen.

Plamil Foods actively markets to a variety of consumer groups, one of the largest being those who are food intolerant, either self-diagnosed or diagnosed by a medical practitioner. Other markets include those allergic to certain ingredients and the ethical consumers who are seeking fair trade, organic, sustainable, and vegan products.

"When we're marketing outside the vegan community, we don't focus so heavily on the vegan aspect," says managing director Adrian Ling. "The product and marketing material will carry a vegan logo but it won't be so heavily marketed in that direction. For instance, we manufacture no-added-sugar chocolate and most people seeking no-added-sugar chocolate don't care whether it's vegan or not. We'd like to sell our vegan products to as many people as possible, and if that means they're buying a vegan product without knowing it, that doesn't necessarily matter, and, since we're a vegan company, it means that person isn't purchasing a non-vegan product from another company."

Interestingly, Lagusta Yearwood finds that the best way to attract vegans to her products is *not* to market to them. "My theory is that I quit doing formal animal rights activism in order to focus on making vegan food, and if I want it to be my activism, I can't just have vegans eating it—we need non-vegans to be eating our chocolates," she says. "So we don't market to vegans, though vegans are sneaky, and we always find out about good vegan food and tell all our vegan friends. So, it works both ways. I love that vegans love our stuff, because I love vegans. But in order to feel like the business is doing what it should be doing, we downplay the vegan aspect of it."

Titbits Catering takes a similar approach, with an emphasis on vibrant, visual marketing to attract non-vegans.

Sometimes it's useful to look outside your industry for creative promotional ideas. "Whether your business sells a product or service, it's important to do benchmarking and understand what other people are doing who are in highly competitive markets to figure out what you can do to differentiate yourself," says Stephanie Redcross. "If you sell skincare products, you may think about benchmarking against eyeglasses. Or look at the car industry. Sometimes it's helpful to look somewhere totally different because you'll start to see a more creative perspective. Push yourself away from that tunnel vision that sometimes occurs when you're stuck in your particular industry—the kind of thinking that says, 'This is what we do in skincare, and that's it.'"

Storytelling and Emotions

As Donna Oakes-Jones pointed out earlier, explaining to customers the story behind your products is a smart marketing strategy. It can touch people and warm them to your brand, conquering concerns they may have around price, health, ethics, or other issues.

Addiction Food's Georgie Campbell agrees. "A lot of people are constantly looking for new, innovative ideas, or looking for the product that's completely different from what else is on the market. So offering a point of difference and also telling the story behind the products generates their interest. Our really loyal customers have got to know us and what we're about," says Campbell.

As we'll see in the upcoming chapter on PR and media, finding the stories in your business is the way to get journalists to feature you in their editorial coverage. This is free promotion that would ordinarily cost you hundreds, thousands, tens of thousands, or even hundreds of thousands of dollars, so it's worth not underestimating the power of stories in your marketing.

Use stories in your marketing to stir up emotions. Remember, we buy on emotion and justify our purchases with logic.

To connect with your potential customers on an emotional level and build rapport with them so they trust you requires an understanding of the five senses—also known as modalities.

We all navigate our way through the world using these modalities. Each person is typically dominant in one particular modality. If you can communicate with them using words, phrases and language that resonate with them, they're more likely to feel that you 'get' them and will buy from you.

The five senses or modalities are:

• What we see (visual modality)
• What we hear (auditory modality)
• What we smell (olfactory modality)
• What we feel (kinesthetic modality)
• What we taste (gustatory modality)

We mostly use our **visual, auditory, and kinesthetic** modalities when making sense of our world. For example, something may *feel* good or *ring a bell* or we *see* what someone means.

Some people are also what in Neuro Linguistic Programming (NLP) terms called Auditory Digital (AD) which means they want to know how something works. AD people tell themselves things and have a lot of self-talk.

When we understand these modalities—from both a personal perspective on how we process information and a view of how other people navigate the world around them—it means we can match and mirror their modalities to build rapport with them via our marketing materials.

Visual people
People who are primarily visual *see* the world by constructing or remembering mental pictures. If you ask them to imagine or

remember something, they'll create or recall an image in their mind, often in great detail and color. They'll mostly use and respond to words or phrases like:

Look
See
Focus
Paint a picture
View
Bright
Bird's-eye view
Clear
Watch
Take a peek
Sight for sore eyes
An eyeful
Short-sighted
Snapshot
Reveal

Visual people often shallow breathe from the top of their lungs and will tend to look up a lot. They often sit forward in their chair. If someone is very put together, fashion wise, they'll likely be navigating the world primarily through their visual modality. They memorize things by seeing pictures and are less distracted by noise. They often have trouble remembering verbal instructions as their minds tend to wander. They generally learn best by writing or drawing. A visual person will be interested in how your product or service *looks*.

Auditory people

Auditory people navigate the world through sound. They listen to what is around them and construct their thoughts and feelings based on what they hear. An auditory person will mostly use and respond to words like:

Sounds
Resonates
Rings a bell
Voice an opinion
Clear as a bell
Loud and clear
Music to my ears
Be all ears
Hear
Tune out
Tell
Listen
On another note
Amplify

Auditory people breathe slightly more deeply than visual people, from the middle of their chests. Because they hear sounds, they're easily distracted by noise. They're good at remembering verbal instructions and can repeat things back to you easily. They learn best by listening and usually enjoy music and talking on the phone. They like to be told how they're doing and respond to and are sensitive to voice tone. Auditory people will want to know what you have to *say* about your product or service and how it *sounds*.

Kinesthetic people
Kinesthetic people are the touchy-feely types. They navigate their world through physical contact, feelings, and intuition. They'll have and respect their "gut feeling." They'll mostly use and respond to words like:
Feel
Intuition
Gut feeling
Grasp

Touch
Get hold of
Tap into
Make contact
Get to grips
Firm foundation
Smooth
Heated argument
Pull some strings
Concrete

Kinesthetic people will typically breathe and speak very deeply and slowly. They're likely to stand more closely to others because they're comfortable with physical contact. They learn and memorize by doing something—to "get a feel" for it. They'll be interested in your product or service if it *feels* right.

Auditory digital people
AD people have a lot of self-talk going on. They'll spend quite a bit of time talking to themselves. They mostly like and respond to words such as:
Outcome
Systems analysis
Good sense
Data
Process of
ROI
Methodologies
Direction
KPIs
Foreseeable issues
Procedures

AD people are all about the specifics. They want to know the *details* of your product or service and how it works.

To get engagement from potential and existing customers, you need to appeal to the different modalities. Do this by using language in your marketing materials that comprise visual, auditory, kinesthetic, and auditory digital words and phrases.

We're naturally curious creatures and will engage with anything that stops us in our tracks. It could be visually striking, a piece of music, a song, or unusual sound. It could make us feel happy, sad, moved, uplifted, angry, motivated. As a business owner, you must learn to know people and what makes them tick, so you can figure out how to draw their attention to your brand.

"If you have a shop where people physically walk in, you must have something at the front of the shop or a sign standing on the sidewalk that will make people stop and take notice," says Ron Prasad. "Study the psychology of consumers in order to decide what they want. Put yourself in their shoes and ask, 'What will draw me into this shop?'"

Diversify Your Marketing Strategies

Just as marketing using only one modality limits who you can reach, so too is focusing all your efforts on one single platform. If that platform disappears or stops working, your leads dry up and sales plummet.

An example of this is organic Google listings. Many business owners, including solo practitioners, had a free ride for several years by being featured on the first page of Google for their product or service at no cost. Then Google shifted the goal posts massively, introducing algorithm update after algorithm update, penalizing businesses left, right, and center, and catapulting them out of the search engine listings. It left many businesses devastated and scrambling to find alternative ways to attract customers.

Be across different platforms and find out which ones work best for you. People start to take notice of you and your brand when they see you regularly in different places. In marketing terms this is known as a "touch" and consumers generally need at least seven "touches" before they start to consider you of interest and worthy of their time in exploring further.

"The way people respond isn't when they're notified 15 times on Facebook about your product or service," says Ella Nemcova. "The way they respond is when they saw out of the corner of their eye a notification, and they overheard someone talking about you; then they saw your name pop up somewhere on a poster of something you're sponsoring, and they went to an event, and you were there. Do everything you can to be on people's radar because, when they experience you in that way, then they really listen; you've become a celebrity to them."

Eco-Vegan Gal's Whitney Lauritsen agrees. "I work hard to 'be everywhere,' especially on social media and, over time, I've become known in the vegan community," she says.

That said, it's also important not to burn out, and to implement strategies that make the most efficient use of your time and resources, warns David Benzaquen. "Ask yourself, 'Who do you most need to reach and where can you reach them?' If you sell a vegan food product and your goal is to get non-vegans to buy it, are you not better off frequenting communities outside of your own? If your service is targeted at adults over the age of 65, wouldn't you be better off marketing offline?" he says.

Allocate a Marketing Budget

One of the major mistakes aspiring, new, and existing business owners make is failure to invest enough in marketing. It's tempting, particularly when starting a business, to plough all your money into premises, equipment, expensive software, and so on and leave little to nothing to promote the business.

While there are ways to market for free, increasingly it's now the case, even on social media, that you need to pay for results. The more you can invest in your marketing, the more return you'll get.

Yaoh owner and VegFestUK co-organizer Tim Barford explains how investment in marketing is crucial to the success or otherwise of the festivals his team puts on across the UK each year. "We always market our shows really well now. I remember, there was one occasion we certainly didn't and we noticed it. We could tell by the number of visitors—it was bad; there were fewer people. We hadn't done a proper marketing job and it showed," admits Barford. "Fortunately, we realized that and we made sure that the next year we did a double effort. Now we spend up to 40 percent of our budget on marketing, and that's why we get 10,000-plus people to the Olympia exhibition center in London because we *really* market our shows very widely."

Barford knows that, for vegan businesses, hiring a booth or stall at festivals is a key component of their own marketing strategy, requiring resources, time, and money. This acts as an incentive for the VegFestUK team to bring large numbers of visitors to the festivals.

"They know we're spending tens of thousands of pounds on marketing and making sure these people come to their stall," says Barford. "We understand that with stall hire, staff, travel and accommodation costs, small business owners may have to spend up to around £500 or £600 in total, but if you're getting back £1,000 just with sales for the day and lots of flyers are out, you're meeting your customers and getting your brand right in front of thousands of people, that's a good-value show. One or two people would prefer things to be cheaper, but then we wouldn't be able to spend so much on marketing, and we wouldn't have so many people there."

Eric Lindstrom, founder of ThankTank Creative, an award-winning design and marketing firm in New York, advises small business owners to put aside 20 percent of their gross annual revenue for marketing and advertising. "Fees for professional agencies range from expensive to more expensive when factored against the immediate expenses of operating a business.

I've found that, unfortunately, many businesses spend the most marketing dollars for their 'going out of business' sales. Largely, this could be avoided by investing marketing dollars in your business before it gets to that stage," says Lindstrom.

Working with Marketing Professionals

Should you hire a marketing professional? It's tempting for business owners to want to palm off the marketing to someone else while they focus on doing what they're good at, and this makes sense. As David Benzaquen points out: "Spending money on trying to sell a product or service without knowing where, to who, and how to sell or market that product as efficiently and effectively as possible is much more expensive in the long-run."

However, there are some caveats. First, marketing coaches and consultants are everywhere. In many places, there are no regulations and anyone can set themselves up as an expert, take your money, and deliver zero results.

As with hiring any professional, you must do your due diligence. "Ask any potential marketing partner, whether it's a graphic designer, a digital marketer, a field marketer, or anyone else, what tools they use to develop the strategy that underpins their work, what factors weigh in their choice of tactics, and what metrics they use to measure their success," advises Benzaquen. "Work with your marketing partners to set clear, definable timelines for deliverables, budgets, and measurable goals."

Lindstrom emphasizes the importance of hiring professionals with the same ethical values as you. "Of course, there are countless agencies out there that disappoint, but working with like-minded businesses usually equates a successful partnership," he says. "Discuss terms and request shorter contracts. With ThankTank Creative, we offer a three-month option and six-month option, which allows for plenty of time to see how well we work with our clients, and allows them to be more flexible with long-term marketing decisions."

Of course, working with a professional is a two-way street, and you must be prepared to play your part. This requires being willing to learn, be open to new strategies, and taking action on them. "There is nothing more frustrating than investing time in a client who decides that they like their current model better, even when the market shows that it's not as effective," says Benzaquen.

Even if you decide to hire a marketing professional, it's still a good idea for you as the business owner to have a basic understanding of marketing, particularly what's working right now, because things change so quickly. What may have been bringing you a ton of leads or sales six months ago may result in you getting a 'Google slap' or 'Facebook slap'.

Many business owners have had their Facebook accounts suspended for activities that the platform ignored for months or years but then decided those activities were no longer acceptable. Their accounts were shut down and some business owners have not been able to reinstate them. This means they lost their pages and the fans they worked hard to collect. A good marketing professional will keep up to date with the most cutting-edge strategies, but you'd to be wise to keep yourself in the loop too.

Test and Measure

So, you've come up with your marketing strategies, allocated a budget, and started spending. That's all good, but you have to measure your results; otherwise, you may be wasting money on avenues that aren't working. It's dead money. Sometimes, you'll spend a chunk of money on marketing or advertising, but the results were nowhere near what you hoped for. Rather than think of this as a failure, see it as a learning curve and don't repeat it.

Not every single marketing effort will yield fantastic results. It's a case of test and measure. Sometimes, a particular marketing strategy doesn't work effectively because you haven't implemented it correctly. This is particularly true of platforms involving complex algorithms, such as Google or Facebook. If you don't know what you're doing, your results will be miserable and you may be tempted to throw in the towel and declare that "Facebook marketing doesn't work." But those who take the time to figure out what does work can clean up on the platform.

Fortunately, these platforms offer metrics, so you can see what results you're getting and how much a lead or sale is costing you. This allows you to change your strategy, or, if something is working particularly well, do more of that.

The only way to find out, for example, if your customers respond well or poorly to you increasing the amount of emails you send them, is to try it and see. You may be worried about 'harassing' them, but, sometimes, you have to bite the bullet and give it a go.

"Many times people tend to forget about standard testing techniques. Their error is in *assuming* they're harassing their customers, so they pull back their marketing," says Stephanie Redcross. "Every quarter, you should be testing something within your marketing strategy to see if you need to push the envelope a little bit more, or if you need to be pulling back."

In the next chapter we'll look at the use of the 'V' word in your marketing: How much, if at all, should the word *vegan* feature in your marketing materials? The final chapters will delve deeper into different types of marketing.

Meanwhile, keep in mind these key components summarized by David Benzaquen for making your business stand out through your marketing in a positive way:

- Understand who your audience is and what *they* are looking for through research and good listening.
- Understand what your competitors are doing and do something different.
- Speak and act with authenticity, humility, and integrity.
- Know what you're best at and focus on that, rather than trying to meet everyone's desires or needs.

- Use the communication tools that most effectively represent your product or service to the right audience. In a time of so much clutter, how can you spark interest through different sensorial experiences? Can you use audio? Video? Smell? Taste? Storytelling?
- Hone your message to the most essential and impactful elements.

Chapter 7

Should You Use the 'V' Word in Your Branding & Marketing?

How much should you use the word *vegan* in your marketing or even your business name, if at all? Is *plant-strong* or *plant-powered* or *plant-based* better, to avoid scaring people off? Or should we be bold in our use of the 'V' word to reclaim it from its negative stereotyping of being the domain of bland, dowdy, cult-following extremists?

The answer is: it depends on who your market is.

"Are you trying to target people who identify with the word 'vegan'? Some people *have* to see the word to buy," says Vegan Mainstream's Stephanie Redcross. "Similarly, some products nowadays will state, 'This is a product for people who have diabetes.' So people who have diabetes will specifically look for those products. It doesn't mean another product won't work for them, but it brings them comfort or assurance to see that statement or logo on the packaging."

Deciding on a name and marketing copy for your business shouldn't be about whether or not to include the word *vegan,* but more about what your business is and what your brand stands for.

Those Who Say "Yes" to the 'V' Word

For some business owners, there's no question about using the word *vegan* in their branding and marketing. They see it as a form of activism and pride.

"If it scares people away, then good riddance," asserts Cocoon Apothecary's Jessica Burman. "I don't want anti-vegan people buying my products. Since we're already in the natural, organic realm, our clientele is quite used to the word 'vegan' and they appreciate it in beauty products."

For Elizabeth Olsen, veganism was the reason she created her eponymous shoe company, Olsenhaus. "I have nothing to fear or hide from. People told me in the beginning not to put the word 'vegan' in the logo, but it didn't even cross my mind to not have it there. I think it helped the company by separating it from other companies and making it stand out. I think it also gave us respect from the vegan community for being so open about our veganism," says Olsen.

Ethical Wares's Mike Newman believes it's important to make clear the company's vegan values. "If it puts people off, so be it. We are what we are and would never pretend to be otherwise. An ethical business should reflect the ethics of those running it. Our business is an extension of our beliefs," says Newman.

Cow Jones Industrials's Donna Oakes-Jones agrees. "The word 'vegan' is front and center on my online shop and it was the same when I had my physical shop. I loved having that word on my shop's sign. To me, it created an oasis for those who were looking for vegan products," says Oakes-Jones.

Le Petite Spa's Mary Prenon takes a similar approach. "Right away, you're telling people that your spa is different. It's special. I think people—especially those who aren't familiar with vegan products—are going to want to find out more," says Prenon.

Ayana Organics's Samantha Crosby sees providing vegan-labeled and marketed products as a form of affirmative action. "Not everyone will buy a product because it's vegan, but, in my opinion, it won't put people off. More importantly, vegan customers will only buy vegan-labeled products. We live in a non-vegan world and I market my products as vegan with pride. The niche is growing and will continue to grow every day," says Crosby.

Vegan Proteins's Giacomo Marchese and Dani Taylor are also proud to use the term, both in their company's name, as well as marketing collateral. "We aren't just 'plant-based'; we're vegan and proud of it," says Taylor. "Also, people have been fairly aggressive in their questioning of us, prior to starting our business, about how we could ever build muscle as vegans. We want to make it clear that we *are* vegan and we *do* have muscles, and many of our customers feel the same way. By putting the word 'vegan' in our name, maybe we do alienate some people, but we intrigue just as many, and that's what we're looking to do. This business was started to spread awareness about what's possible as a vegan."

Hemp company Yaoh was stamped with the vegan logo on its products from its inception, long before owner Tim Barford was running VegFestUK events. It was a decision that has seen Yaoh retain a loyal community of vegan consumers. "It's been very positive, being identified as a vegan product. Yaoh is a body care and food product in the natural products arena. We were loud and proud vegan but that was because the market we were identifying with was always vegan-friendly, especially the people who were deciding whether to take the product in their stores. Many of them would be either vegan or vegetarian, or certainly vegan- and vegetarian-friendly," says Barford.

The sign above the door at Ms. Cupcake in London's Brixton proudly proclaims, "The Naughtiest Vegan Cakes in Town," yet makes it clear that all are welcome in the store. "We don't hide the fact that we are vegan, but we make cake for everyone," says owner Mellissa Morgan. "We certainly wouldn't say to someone when they walk through the door, 'Hello, are you a vegan?' So I guess it's possible that someone may not see the sign or the vegan and animal rights literature on our shelves. They just see amazing cake, and that's fine.

"When we started the business, I think we'd been open a few weeks and the local people were very curious and they were coming in, sampling the products and buying cakes. After a few weeks, a woman came in and asked, 'So what is this 'vegan' you put in all your cakes?' It was funny, and, to me, that meant we're doing it right because, although she knew that it had something to do with this vegan thing, which she didn't understand, it wasn't stopping her from buying the cakes," says Morgan.

Rubyfruit owners Amanda Solomons and Simone Bateman felt it would be a disservice to their clientele not to have the word *vegan* in their branding, despite friends and family warning them against it. "To do otherwise would have felt like we were hiding our passion. It's what we are; we are a vegan business," says Solomons. "Also, we had to be comfortable in labeling our business clearly so that any confusion with customers was prevented as much as possible. We then had something to fall back on if people still took issue with elements such as having soy milk in their coffee. Honesty, passion, and authenticity works for us. It might alienate some potential customers, but others respond well, and it's what feels right to us."

Bounty Burgers's Loren Lembke refused to bow down to pressure from family to use the term *meat-free* because she's on a mission to make the term *vegan* a household name. It's written in large letters on the product's packaging and even explains what the word means. "I thought it probably will put some people off, but that's going to be their problem because I'm not here to be popular. I want people to think about what they're consuming," says Lembke.

Jivamukti Yoga's Sharon Gannon has "never shied away" from using the word *vegan*. "We never felt afraid that promoting veganism would impact upon our students negatively. We're a school, committed to education. People know that and they come to us to be educated about all aspects of yoga. We teach veganism as one of those aspects," says Gannon.

GUNAS's Sugandh G. Agrawal is on a mission to connect fashion and veganism in a positive way. With her unique and affordable designs, her handbags are particularly popular among vegan consumers. "Veganism is the foundation of my brand. The vegan market has strong opinions about not choosing animal products or animal byproducts and I have the same kind of strong feelings, so I have to use the word 'vegan'," says Agrawal. "And I also think that a lot of times, people think when you say, 'vegan,' it's just the food but it's also fashion. It's not only what you put *in* your body; it's also what you put *on* your body."

ESPE's Eva Fung believes that with non-food products, people who are indifferent about vegan items will only care about the design, quality, and value. "People who are vegan-conscious will focus on the ethical aspect as well. We win on both fronts!" says Fung.

Bed and Broccoli's Nikki Medwell uses the word *vegan* in the bed and breakfast's marketing, but doesn't "overuse" it and makes a point of balancing it with the term *pre-vegans* instead of *non-vegans*. "While we promote ourselves as Australia's first vegan B&B on our website, we also say, 'If you're not vegan, it doesn't matter; come anyway, experience the food, meet the rescued animals,'" says Medwell. "I know for a fact that our Facebook page has so many pre-vegans following us, which is incredible, and it's because I include them in our journey—I don't ostracize them."

Vx's Rudy Penando makes a point of associating the word *vegan* with other words that don't usually come to mind. "We were the first place in the UK using the term 'vegan junk food'. It gets the attention from carnists and vegans alike," says Penando.

Also getting the attention of non-vegans is Swami Hennessy-Mitchell's CocoLuscious coconut ice cream, which has become the ice cream of choice at many paleo and other cafés in Australia. "I'm proud to be vegan and proud of what I've created. I don't shy away from the vegan label at all, and have it on my websites and on the packaging. I initially created my products for the vegan market. It's been almost by accident that it's taken off the way it has. I love knowing that people who are consuming diets high in animal products are also buying CocoLuscious and being exposed to the vegan logo," says Hennessy-Mitchell.

Ella Nemcova admits that she made inaccurate assumptions about many people's perceptions of the word *vegan* when coining the name of her brand The Regal Vegan, but believes the term will come into its own in the future. "I came from a marketing background, and, at that time, 'vegan' was never scary to me. Looking back, I'm not sure that I would put 'vegan' in the title because it's polarizing. I think a lot of people avoid using the word because they don't want people to think that it doesn't taste good, and this is a perception of veganism that perhaps will be a little slower to turn around, but I recommend that people play a long game. I think that vegan is in the future for food and seeing 'vegan' on your packaging tells people right away, 'Here's our ethics in five letters.' And they speak volumes," says Nemcova.

Communicating your vegan values is a way to establish what you will or won't do as a business.

"We're very forthcoming about being vegan, working for animal rights non-profits and campaigns, books and films about animal issues, vegan products, and so on," says Evolotus PR's Kezia Jauron. "I've passed up business opportunities with companies whose products aren't 100 percent vegan because I'm not comfortable with that ethically. I'd like us to move away from the idea that vegan is scary. Veganism is more and more acknowledged and understood. So many people today have a vegan in their family, their office, their church, or their kid's classroom. Also, there are vegans working at all levels of media, even though they're sometimes in the closet, from top producers at Fox News and MSNBC to reporters at newspapers nationwide who are hungry for good stories to bring to their editors. If vegan entrepreneurs aren't willing to use the term, who will?" says Jauron.

Some vegan business owners start out brandishing the word vegan *everywhere, but then change tactics.*
"If you asked me seven years ago, I would've gone for the whole 'Vegan is clever; it's niche.' Now, I've completely turned around

and say that, unless we're at a vegan expo, a vegan festival, or something like that, we don't use the word anymore," says Addiction Food's Georgie Campbell. "In our experience, unfortunately, too many people take it on board that you're accusing them of being wrong, and it's been quite nasty sometimes. So, I'm very careful how we use that word. It's about educating people, slowly but surely, and I just don't think the word 'vegan' is the one to use. Say 'plant-based', say 'sustainable', say 'compassionate', say whatever you want, but 'vegan' just seems to be a bit of a controversial and misunderstood label.

Nicobella's Nichole Dandrea was also passionate about the 'V' word when she first started her chocolate business, then changed her approach after listening to her clientele. "When I first started out, everything said 'vegan' and I was proudly shouting it out to everybody and I was scaring so many people away," recalls Dandrea. "It was a little frustrating because it's just a dark chocolate company, and a lot of people would come up and say, 'I'm not vegan; I can't have it.' And instead of getting frustrated, I had to figure out a better way to get these people to try it and educate them, because the goal was to bring more people on board with plant-based eating.

"So I changed the approach, and, instead of plastering 'vegan' everywhere and letting people know before they even tried the chocolate, I would just tell them it's dark chocolate. Sometimes, I'd say it's healthy, or sometimes, I'd just say, 'Would you like to try some dark chocolate?' And once they tried it, then I'd tell them it's vegan, and they'd most often be pleasantly surprised," says Dandrea.

Vegan Style's Justin Mead also questions whether the inclusion of the word *vegan* in his company's name limits its appeal outside the vegan community. "It's definitely been a challenge in some areas because it puts some people off. I'm proud to call myself a vegan. I always, first and foremost, wanted to service the vegan community with our business. So, for me, it was a little bit of a no-brainer to put the word in our name, but, in retrospect, it does limit you. Yet we need to be proud of the term and put it out there in the community and not be ashamed of it," says Mead, who in early 2015 introduced another shoe line called Zette. The new line has a wider appeal by not featuring the word *vegan* in its name, yet still retains vegan values. The brand's individual shoe lines are named after cats that Mead and his partner have rescued over the years.

On the flip side, there are business owners who avoided including **vegan** *in their names and marketing to begin with, but now embrace the term.*

"If I were starting again now, I'd use the word 'vegan' everywhere, and not because it's a niche market but because I want the word out there as much as possible, because the more the word's out there, the more acceptance it gets," says The Cruelty Free Shop's Jessica Bailey. "Things that are familiar aren't scary, so the more people see the word 'vegan', the more it becomes normal and people don't react badly to it. So now I wear my vegan t-shirts and if I were starting the business today, I'd probably call it the The Vegan Shop or something similar."

222 Veggie Vegan's Ben Asamani has come to a similar conclusion to Bailey. Few people understood what vegan cuisine was 10 years ago in London when he first opened the restaurant, so he made it clear on the signage that it was a vegetarian restaurant, adding the terms *veggie* and *vegan* to attract both these markets.

"Some people still think we shouldn't use the word 'vegan', but I think we've moved on now that people are beginning to understand and accept it. I'm doing some interior designing and when I'm finished I'm going to put on the outside, '222 Vegan Cuisine.' I will not compromise that anymore," says Asamani.

Those Who Say "No" to the 'V' Word
Some vegan business owners steer clear of using the word *vegan*

in their branding and marketing.

For Lagusta Yearwood of Lagusta's Luscious, not using the word is a form of stealth activism. "We're happiest when people have no idea that things are vegan or organic until long after they've tasted them, because that means we're changing people's minds about how food that's produced in an ethical way tastes. As a former animal rights activist, I don't necessarily want vegans eating my confections, because vegans are already eating vegan food. I want non-vegans eating what I make, because that means they're eating fewer animals," says Yearwood.

Iku Wholefood's franchisee Kendall Hayes avoids using the word *vegan* because she believes it can be interpreted as "too extreme" and is likely to put the company's mostly mainstream customers off. "We already have people walk past our stores saying, 'Oh, too healthy.' So we avoid promoting that we are vegan as well as 'healthy.' We just can't afford to lose customers because they think our food is 'weird'! It's really important to define your market and know your customers. For us, as retail business owners in the financial district of Sydney, we believe it's important to focus on the health benefits that wholefood offers busy corporates. I also like to use the word 'ethical' over 'vegan' because if people are interested, they'll ask what is ethical about our food. That way, they've invited the conversation and we can then discuss not only health but also the environmental and animal welfare issues," says Hayes.

Cruelty Free Super's Lee Coates also decided against including the word *vegan* in the business's name, in order to encompass people, animals, and planet in its mission. "We thought of calling the business Vegan Super, but we believe 'cruelty-free' is more holistic. When marketing to vegans, we make it clear it's a vegan product and we follow vegan standards, but we want to encourage non-vegans to join because they might be interested in human rights or the environment and then, as with staff, they learn about the animal welfare issues as part of their membership.

Education, rather than force-feeding, leads to more sustainable change in people," says Coates.

Tim Barford, who saw success with the use of the word *vegan* in the marketing of his hemp business, Yaoh, had the opposite experience with VegFestUK. The event started out as the Bristol Vegan Fayre, but the organizers found the term alienated non-vegans. "As a festival, we were trying to appeal to the mainstream. We wanted to attract people who were of no particular dietary persuasion or background who could come and have a veggie burger, feel the vibe, have a good time, and get a positive introduction to the vegan lifestyle through fantastic stalls. But we found that, instead of our audiences growing, they were beginning to dwindle. So, we did some research and learned that people thought because we were a vegan festival, we were only for vegans," Barford explains. "Vegetarians, especially, found our event quite off-putting, and, since we changed the name and became VegFestUK, it completely changed the dynamic. It's a lot more inclusive. The vegetarians and the flexitarians now find our shows much more attractive."

While the name change was unpopular with some vegans, who accused the organizers of watering down the vegan message, Barford argues that VegFestUK opens up the vegan lifestyle to far greater numbers. In 2014, the London VegFestUK saw 9,000 attendees, resulting in the festival upgrading to the largest hall at the prestigious Olympia exhibition center for the 2015 event. "We do our best to try to be inclusive and make it clear that we are a vegan event. Everything on display or for sale at the events is vegan, but, outside of that, we're not making any judgments; everyone's welcome. There may be a day when they want to become vegan, so, until then, we want them to come and enjoy the fun," says Barford.

Nacheez's Ilsa Hess chose to use the term *dairy-free* instead of *vegan* because of the poor reputation of vegan cheeses as tasting "horrible." But although the term doesn't appear on the front of her label, Hess added the word *vegan* above the list of ingredients and has a "Why Vegan?" section on her website. "I wanted to give people a place where they can go and learn more about the animal-based dairy industry and why I chose to go vegan," says Hess.

Health practitioner Heather Lounsbury wants to appeal to a mainstream market for her acupuncture and Chinese Medicine services, hence *vegan* is not prominent in her branding or marketing. "I sense people are still turned off by the word, unfortunately. I steer away from it because I want as many people to come to me as possible without any preconceived ideas. I feel that, with what I do for a living, it's best to not put that right up front because it could turn people away that potentially may become vegan or vegetarian. Over the years, pretty much all my patients are eating fewer animal products across the board and many of them have gone vegan and vegetarian. I'm honest with my patients—if they ask me, I'm very open about it and I don't hold anything back, but it's not the first thing that comes out of my mouth," says Lounsbury.

Hypnotherapist, naturopath and business mindset coach Dr Tracie O'Keefe takes a similar approach to Lounsbury to attract people who would otherwise come nowhere near her practice. "We don't advertise as being vegan and we don't declare that to people when they enter our business. We simply state that we use cruelty-free products and operate according to plant-based eating philosophies. Interestingly, I have several sheep and cattle farmers who came to see me who then became vegan for health reasons," says O'Keefe.

While for some business owners, the 'V' word is an either/or choice, others employ it strategically depending on the context.
Author, consultant and vegan lifestyle coach JL Fields created her business name as JL Fields Consulting, LLC, and her diverse programs and cooking classes, including her popular blog

JL Goes Vegan, come under this umbrella. It's a strategic approach designed to bring as many people into a conversation with her, without immediately scaring them away with the 'V' word.

Fields's cooking and coaching services website is jlgoesvegan. com. She was advised to consider omitting *vegan* but she wanted prospective clients to be clear about her mission and vision.

"I'm an ethical vegan and I want people to know what they are getting into, so I don't call myself plant-strong or plant-powered because that's not how I identify. But because I do a considerable amount of corporate consulting, I chose JL Fields Consulting, LLC as my legal business name and consulting website," says Fields.

However, she doesn't hide the fact she's vegan on her consulting site, with a section linking to her services as a vegan coach and cook. "I have to think strategically and consider, when I'm meeting someone, what is going to encourage them to continue a conversation with me? When they do go to the site, they're still going to find out who I am, but I might have softened the blow a little bit. I'm conscious of the term because I don't want it to alienate people, but I don't hide it from them. So, I make sure that no matter how people meet me, they'll find out what I'm really about," says Fields.

Titbits Catering's Paula Young avoids using the word *vegan* when she's promoting her pop-up restaurant. "I find that it puts people off," she says. "Also when I run a market stall, I don't have a big banner saying 'vegan.' I've found that most people would walk past at the sight of the 'vegan' word. People eat with their eyes and are drawn in by the yummy feast before them. At this stage, many realize the food is vegetarian and happily buy a plate."

Young does, however, state on the company website that Titbits is a vegan catering company, registered with The Vegan Society. "Vegans, in my experience, are used to looking at labels that clearly indicate all food is suitable for vegans. And I feel that once people have tried the food and are aware we are a vegan company, there's no point in hiding the fact. It's also important that anyone specifically looking for vegan catering find us in an internet search," she says.

Social media consultant and owner of the popular Australian website vivalavegan.com, Leigh-Chantelle, recommends using a term that's likely to have longevity. "A lot of people are relying on niche marketing at the moment, whether it's raw, paleo, or vegan, so it depends on whether it's something that's still going to be relevant in 10 years. Is it cruelty-free? Plant-based? If it's something that you can see will still be around, then use whatever term you think is right for your audience," says Leigh-Chantelle.

Nowadays, vegans are becoming more entrepreneurial, garnering several streams of income from different projects. Some of these may include judicious use of the term *vegan*, while other projects refrain from broadcasting it while still running the businesses according to vegan principles.

Clare Mann, for example, operates a general psychology practice, as well as a specific service providing coaching, psychotherapy, and counseling to vegans. "In the latter, veganism is focused on and mentioned in all promotions, whereas, in the former, it's not mentioned and would only occur if appropriate to discuss from the client's perspective," says Mann.

Mann's communications training business is not branded as being vegan, but all live events and workshops have vegan catering for morning and afternoon tea as well as lunch. "We find this is a great way of teasing in vegan values throughout our company," says Mann.

Melissa Dion takes the approach of using the word *vegan* on the Ecolissa online store and in the company's marketing, but focuses even more on the eco-friendly aspects of the products. "The fact is that most of Ecolissa's customers aren't vegan, and I'm concerned that a stronger message might turn them off," says Dion.

PlantBased Solutions's David Benzaquen says the effectiveness of any word is dependent on who is being reached and with what purpose.

"An effective business owner or advocate for social change—as many of us wear both hats—must put the impact of their image, words, and other identifying characteristics above their own personal preferences. Marrying this awareness with an understanding of who your target audience is creates the foundation for effective messaging. If your business mission is to sell funny and inspiring t-shirts for vegans to wear, then using the word 'vegan' in the brand name may be good targeting. However, if your goal is to reach non-vegans with a product or service, it may be more effective to highlight the offering in a different way, particularly if the audience would be alienated by the word."

Chapter 8
Social Media Marketing

Facebook, Twitter, Instagram, Pinterest, LinkedIn, Google Plus, YouTube—these are just a handful of the most popular social media platforms at the time of writing, with new ones coming on board regularly.

To the busy business owner, it can seem overwhelming, particularly if you feel pressured to maintain accounts on all these different platforms. Where do you find time to create content, post it, as well as interact with commenters, not only on your own content, but also on that of other influencers in your industry?

Vegan Mainstream's Stephanie Redcross recommends keeping your social media efforts to a small number of platforms, rather than trying to manage several in a mediocre way. "You don't have to do it all in the beginning," she advises. "Too many people start off thinking, 'I have to be on *every* social media platform.' But you don't need to be. You might want to *create* the account so you secure the name, but you may not manage it for a year or two years from now. Instead, get some focus. Pick one or two, do them *really* well for six months and then add a third one. Do that well again for another six months. Now you're a year in and then you can add another. There's nothing wrong with having a staggered approach because you're small. It's more important to have impact than to look and feel big," says Redcross.

Social media consultant Leigh-Chantelle, who has more than 100,000 followers on her Viva La Vegan! Google Plus channel, agrees and suggests choosing which social media channels to focus on that are best in line with the nature of your business. "If you have a lot of visuals or if you're a photographer, I suggest you focus on image-based channels such as Pinterest or Instagram. Think about what you're trying to achieve, the kind of content you can create, and where it's best suited," says Leigh-Chantelle.

When you're coming up with ideas for content for your social media sites, remember that you can repurpose it to deliver across different channels. For example, if you make a video on a particular topic and put it on your YouTube channel, you can strip out the audio and turn it into a podcast. You can then have this transcribed and edited and turn it into a blog post or an e-report or checklist.

As we saw in Chapter 6, different people have different sense modalities and consume content in different ways. Some prefer to quickly scan text, while others enjoy listening to audio when driving or walking, and others are far more into watching a video. The more ways you can deliver, the more customers you're likely to pick up. I'm a scanner. If you have a video on your site, you'd best have a transcript or at the very least the key points in text below it, or I'm unlikely to watch the video (unless it has cats in it—then I might!).

What Type of Content to Post
This will depend on your business, but images and text together work well, particularly for visual media such as Facebook, Instagram, and Pinterest. Create your own images—there are a number of online tools that allow you to do this quickly and easily, and you can add your website URL at the bottom. Creating your own "memes" means that when they get shared, they're shown on Facebook as being "your" image, which can lead people not only to your URL but also your Facebook page so you can build followers.

The key with social media is to post valuable and entertaining content that people will enjoy, like, comment on, and share.

Bed and Broccoli's Nikki Medwell finds posts about the rescued animals that live on the land by her bed and breakfast business are most popular, alongside food-related content. "During a hot spell, I froze some corn into a muffin tray with some string, then hung it up on low-hanging branches for the hens. I posted a photo of the hens pecking at and playing with what I called 'cornsicles' on our Facebook page and, within a short period of time, it had gathered many likes and had been shared a substantial amount of times," Medwell recalls. "People loved it and the amount of followers on our page increased shortly after I posted it."

Vegan Style's Justin Mead finds that posts about the foster cats he and his partner take in regularly get more likes and shares than the posts about the shoes the company sells. Yet it's authentic, fun, informational, inspirational content that will keep people coming back to your social media sites and ensure your brand remains top of mind for when they are in the market for your products or services.

"I have one rule with social media: just be myself," asserts Lagusta Yearwood of Lagusta's Luscious. "I try to be true to myself and treat my customers like I want to be treated. I don't talk in commercial-speak to them. I use swear words. I like people like that, so I guess I try to attract customers who like the kinds of things I like."

ESPE's Eva Fung takes a similar approach. "For aspiring vegan business owners, I would recommend talking to customers about what you believe in and how your product or service achieves or furthers your cause," says Fung.

Constant "hard sell" of your products or services isn't going to cut it. People are put off by this approach. It doesn't mean you can't promote your wares; you just have to mix it up with a lot of valuable and interesting content, with the occasional promotional post.

Don't be afraid to share other people's content on your social media channels. You'll keep your visitors happy, and there's a good chance that those other people will share your content, so it's a win-win-win.

Build Your Tribe

The main goal with social media should be to interact with your visitors, who may be existing or potential customers. It's not about broadcasting your content, then disappearing. It's essential that you monitor any comments you receive and respond accordingly.

It's also a good idea to engage by leaving comments on posts by influencers in your industry or potential collaborators, as they're also your tribe. Connecting with them in this way can lead to opportunities for you and your business.

Social media is all about relationships. As we saw in Chapter 4, your business's success depends on the quality of the relationships you build. Social media offers you unprecedented access to existing and potential customers, allowing you to talk directly to them and solicit their feedback. You get to find out what they love (or don't) about your products or services, which gives you the opportunity to improve or create additional items. If you're a coach or service provider, you get to ask them what their challenges and needs are.

"Social media is a way to give your business an edge," says Vx's Rudy Penando. "Vx and Secret Society of Vegans are present on most popular social networks. We're particularly active on Instagram, Facebook, Twitter, in that order. We're also on Tumblr, Vine, Snapchat, and Kik. I really enjoy posting and I think it's a good way to gain popularity. We get a lot of interaction and engagement that way as we're pretty quick at answering comments or messages. It's very important. Social media is the new 'customer service,'" says Penando.

Veggie Grill's T.K. Pillan agrees. "The number one rule of marketing is making sure you're delivering to everybody who comes into your business so that they become word-of-mouth advocates. Facebook, Twitter, and Instagram, which are the platforms we're most active on, are just ways to amplify word of mouth. The only way to create good word of mouth is to make sure you continue to provide a compelling experience," says Pillan.

Eco-Vegan Gal's Whitney Lauritsen has built a social media following of over 150,000 at the time of writing. She made a commitment to "be everywhere," particularly in the early stages of her content-producing business. "Social media is the most effective form of marketing for me because it allows me to connect directly with others and add value to their lives. Facebook and YouTube have the most audience interaction and I understand the strategies on how to use them. These platforms generate the most traffic to my site."

Lauritsen's final point is important. The aim of social media, in addition to interacting with your audience, is to drive them to your website, where they can learn about your products or services. Sharing a link to a useful, entertaining blog post on your social media platform, for example, requires people to click through to your site, where they can read it and see what else you offer.

People rarely buy right off the bat when they don't know you. As we learned in Chapter 6, it can take up to seven or more "touches"—the amount of times people need to "see" you—before they'll consider buying from you.

Can You Make Money on Facebook or Other Social Media?
There are arguments on both sides as to how profitable social media is in terms of making sales. Often the sales come later on, as people get to know you and your brand. Once you become known, liked, and trusted, that's when they'll buy from you.

"We tweeted on a Friday afternoon that a particular product was available, and, by Monday morning, we had a number of trade and consumer orders for the product, which we directly attribute to that tweet," says Plamil Foods's Adrian Ling.

Service-based industries can also benefit from social media. Author and vegan lifestyle coach JL Fields says her presence on social media results in bookings for her services because of the honest, authentic, often opinionated posts she makes. "My business is service-oriented, and social media is why I have a good business," says Fields. "I posted a picture of my vegan cowboy boots that I was wearing, and the people who follow me were saying, 'Oh cool, she has vegan cowboy boots.' And for somebody who believes they could never go vegan, they think, 'She's wearing vegan cowboy boots. Who is she?' Then they click through to my website and see they can get vegan lifestyle coaching from me."

Fields offers another example whereby her strong views that vegan doesn't always equate to skinny have led to people signing up for her services. "I've had people reach out to me for individual coaching who said, 'I want to work with you because my doctor told me I need to lose some weight but you're not going to try to make me skinny; you just want me to be healthy.' And they wouldn't know that if not for social media. They wouldn't know that if I didn't go and rant on Twitter!" laughs Fields.

Perhaps one of the best examples of how social media can grow a business is Cruelty Free Super, a vegan, ethical superannuation fund in Australia, started by financial planner Lee Coates while living on the other side of the world in the UK.

Cruelty Free Super was launched and marketed entirely through social media. Its key demographic is young women—not a market traditionally known for prioritizing retirement considerations. "It's been more successful than I think a lot of people thought it would be," says Coates. "One person said to me that we've done everything possible to make it fail! A vegan fund in Australia and Facebook and Twitter are the only marketing strategies. But we're five years old now, and we just hit 600 members and have reached $12 million in the fund."

The company's success is particularly noteworthy, given that money and superannuation are difficult to market as they're not seen as "cool" or "trendy." Coates hired Leigh-Chantelle to help create and share content on the fund's social media sites. Leigh-Chantelle took the approach of producing a range of different types of content. "We've got a lot of videos and podcasts; we also involved a few of our members recently with video interviews and there's a question and answer series that Lee does quite regularly as well," she explains.

Plan Your Content
To avoid the overwhelm that can come with handling your social media content, planning is key.

Leigh-Chantelle advises breaking down tasks and committing to carrying them out regularly. This is particularly true with social media. "Write down every single day what you want to do, whether it's every Monday, Wednesday, and Friday you're going to go on Facebook and post a photo. Or it could be every Tuesday you write new articles and Thursday you create new videos," says Leigh-Chantelle, who also suggests using a scheduling tool such as Hootsuite.

I've tried Hootsuite and Buffer. Currently, I use Buffer, as it's affordable and easy to use. Hootsuite has more features to interact as well as schedule posts, but has a higher learning curve. Some business owners use both, and there are more tools becoming available. So, try them out (most allow you a free trial) to see what works best for you.

You can plan content from as little as a week and as much as a year in advance and anything in between. Once you've planned your content, you can then create it. Sometimes it's easier to create a bunch of content in a block over a certain period—for example, create 12 short YouTube videos in one day, or write five to 10 blog pieces in two days—instead of once or twice a week. If you post the videos monthly, that's a year's worth of content. It depends on your schedule and how you prefer to manage your time.

Pay to Play
In the good old days, social media was free. You could post your content and it would be seen by the majority of your followers. Nowadays, social media platforms are requiring brands to pay

to show and share their content.

At the time of writing, this is particularly the case with Facebook, which shows only a tiny percentage of your followers your posts, unless you pay to boost them or take out an advert. This means if you've spent five years building up a following of 30,000 fans, only up to 3,000 of them (and that's a generous estimate) are likely to see your posts "organically."

This strategy has upset a lot of businesses, but it's the reality of the situation. "You have to put some money aside to focus on advertising, in particular with Facebook," says Leigh-Chantelle. "If you want to get more people to like your page, then you can pay to get more likes from Facebook. That is targeted likes; people who would actually like what you're promoting or what your page stands for. But they might not be interacting with the things you post in a week or a month's time, so then you need to be thinking about putting aside a weekly and monthly budget to promote particular posts."

Tim Barford of Yaoh and VegFestUK doesn't mind paying for social media adverts for commercial purposes, particularly when the return on investment is beneficial. "Facebook actually provides as good a value as any of the platforms we advertise with, if not better. When you want some serious promotion, you've got to pay," says Barford.

Should You Buy Fans or Followers?

This is a hot chestnut. There are pros and cons to "buying" fans or followers. By buying them, I don't mean paying Facebook or Twitter for an ad that shows your page to your target audience so you get more likes or followers, I mean paying third-party providers to supply fake or real but inactive followers.

For under $100, for example, you could "buy" 5,000 or 10,000 fans or followers overnight. It sounds tempting and the arguments for doing so are that you attract more genuine fans by having bought ones to begin with because of the law of social proof. By social proof, I mean if we see someone has 40,000 followers, we believe they're important and must be worthy of following; therefore, we like their page or follow them.

It's a strategy that's employed by celebrities and high-profile politicians, among others, with some media reports claiming that up to 70 percent of fans or followers of many big-name personalities are bought.

The downside is that having a ton of fake or inactive, untargeted followers results in little to no interaction on your social media. The point of having fans and followers is that they engage with your brand; otherwise, having a massive bought following is merely an exercise in narcissism or ego boosting.

Also, social media platforms are starting to penalize accounts with fake or inactive followers and purge those accounts. That means your visible number of followers could drop by thousands suddenly—publicly revealing to any genuine fans that you bought the majority of your audience. It's embarrassing and doesn't look good.

"Nowadays, people are really impatient and want everything to happen *now*; they don't want to put in the work," says Leigh-Chantelle. "But you have to put in the work to make your social media channel successful. I don't think it matters as much how many people are following you online anymore, it's more about the interaction you're getting—and that will come from you creating great content regularly."

Tips on Hiring Social Media Professionals

If you have a budget to hire social media marketing professionals, keep in mind the following:

If they offer to get you 10,000 fans overnight or within a week, run away. Companies like this often prey on unsuspecting business owners, particularly those who aren't tech-savvy and who don't realize the tactics employed are against the social media platforms' terms of services. So, they end up with their accounts suspended or flagged.

Social media is a long-term marketing strategy. To gain genuine fans or followers, you need to consistently create excellent content that's relevant and engaging for your particular audience and allocate a budget to promote certain posts. Make sure you hire someone who understands your business and brand, and, if they're going to create and post content for you, make sure they have the ability to convey your "voice."

Have realistic expectations and make sure you set achievable goals with the professional. "People think they'll just create something, share it on Facebook, 1,000 people will share it, and it will sell 1,000 books or products, but this doesn't happen anymore. The majority of your posts won't go viral," warns Leigh-Chantelle.

Test and Measure

As with any marketing strategy, you must test it and measure it to see how it's performing. There's no point in throwing money at a campaign that's not producing results, and it's no different with social media.

Most of the social media channels have built-in analytics, so you can see how your posts are performing—how many hits they've had, how much interaction and the demographics of the audience. This information is important as it allows you to continue to serve up content that your audience likes and engages with and do less of the content that's not performing well.

This is particularly important when you're running adverts or paying to boost posts. Analyzing the performance regularly enables you to make tweaks to your campaigns so you see a positive return on investment.

Monitoring which social media platforms are performing the best for you also allows you to focus more of your marketing efforts there. "I check in on my analytics regularly and definitely see the value of using them," says Eco-Vegan Gal's Whitney

Lauritsen. "I also generate revenue through YouTube ads, which helps me measure the effectiveness of my videos."

Don't Rely Solely on Social Media

Social media, as we've seen, has its advantages. But be careful not to rely on it as a sole strategy. In marketing circles, the analogy is that creating your communities on social media platforms is like building your house on someone else's land. If they decide to get rid of the land, your home goes with it. They can also choose to evict you any time they like.

Make sure you encourage your fans and followers to sign up to your database via your own website. We'll cover this in more detail in the section on email marketing in an upcoming chapter. For now, think of social media as a complementary marketing strategy rather than a stand-alone one.

Chapter 9
PR & Media

While social media is a great way to interact directly with your fans and followers, getting coverage in independent, niche, and mainstream media outlets can boost your profile and enable your business to grow quickly.

Importance of Media
Here are some of the main advantages of getting media coverage:
- It's affordable. In fact, it's FREE publicity. If you learn how to do your own PR (which is what I teach people), you need little to no marketing budget and don't need to spend thousands or hundreds of thousands of dollars on adverts that offer no guarantee of leads or sales.
- It boosts your credibility. Being featured in the media gives you third-party credibility and endorsement—unlike an advert. Remember that what others say about you or your brand is more important than what you say about your products or services.
- Regular coverage means you become the go-to expert in your industry. This can lead to lucrative opportunities such as paid speaking gigs and joint ventures. Your products and services become synonymous with your field of expertise, leading to more clients, leads, and sales.
- You can reach a range of different types of people or markets by targeting specific media with relevant stories.
- You can get in front of a lot of people fast and for free. Media gets you "out there" much faster than social media, which is a slower and more long-term strategy.

- The media shapes society and cultural thinking—you want to be part of that, particularly when it comes to veganism and ethical living.
- The more media coverage you get, the more you'll continue to get. Journalists consume other media so when they see your name or your product or service come up, they'll often determine if there's another angle they can cover that's specific to their audience.

"When you're first starting out with your business, you've *really* got to put everything out there," says Karin Ridgers, director of Mad Promotions in the UK and host of VeggieVision TV. "Years ago, when I was doing some acting, everybody wanted to learn their lines because they all wanted to be the best actor, and for me, it was the publicity. Because it doesn't matter how good the performance is, it doesn't matter how good the product is, it doesn't matter how good the business is if nobody knows about it."

This was the case for Joy Pierson and Bart Potenza in the early days of building the Candle Cafe business. "The first couple of years were crazy," says Potenza. "We had some business but not enough to cover our expenses. Then we got a very early review in *The New York Times*, and that turned things right around."

In the UK, media has catapulted the growth of the VegFestUK vegan living festivals. Co-organizers Tim Barford and Alan Lee recognize the power that a radio or TV interview on a station with millions of listeners or editorial coverage in a print or online magazine or newspaper can have on the number of people attending their events. "We've had some good high-profile shout-outs, including an interview on *The Gaby Roslin Show* on BBC radio, which has around two million listeners," says Barford. "We've been in the *London Evening Standard* and even *Hello!* magazine." It's this kind of mass exposure that has seen these events grow from a few hundred attendees in a small hall to more than 10,000 people at Olympia in London.

If we want to take veganism to the mainstream and grow our businesses at the same time, public relations (PR) and media coverage are essential. Evolotus PR's Kezia Jauron has helped several food companies expand rapidly. One example is Coconut Bliss, which, at the time, was a mom-and-pop operation selling in select stores in Oregon, Washington, and Northern California. "We worked to get their product to food writers around the country as they grew to national distribution. They went from very small to very well known in less than a year," says Jauron.

Nacheez's Ilsa Hess has experienced monetary gains from her TV appearances. "Each time I was on TV, I noticed a substantial spike in new sales," she says.

What is the Media?

How you define "media" will depend on your age. If you're 30 or older, traditional media probably still comes first to your mind: mainstream TV, radio, newspapers, and magazines. And while these outlets are still major players in the media landscape, they no longer hold the monopoly on content production or information sharing.

The media industry is undergoing a revolution. It's being shaken up or "disrupted" by independent players from bloggers, vloggers, and podcasters to online and digital magazine publishers. Many of these outlets have larger audience numbers than their mainstream counterparts. Social media, the internet and technology have changed the playing field to allow just about anyone to become a publisher.

"People are cutting the cord from TV," explains Jane Velez-Mitchell, best-selling author and renowned US television personality and broadcaster. "Millennials, in particular, watch everything on their computer, phone, or tablet. TV isn't going away anytime soon, but it's in the throes of a massive revolution, and everyone is looking at putting their content online. TV programming online is on the verge of eclipsing regular TV."

Velez-Mitchell, a long-time vegan and animal rights advocate, encourages vegan business owners to take advantage of the new wave of alternative media outlets with large followings to gain exposure for their brands. "Instead of trying to climb Mount Vesuvius, climb other mountains. There are so many new networks emerging online. We need to expand our imagination beyond mainstream traditional TV. The new platforms offer vegan business owners opportunities that they could never have gotten with old-fashioned TV that's predominantly funded by advertisers who aren't vegan. We're now seeing a democratization of media where people can get their message out a thousand different ways on a thousand different platforms, such as *Ecorazzi* or *One Green Planet*," says Velez-Mitchell.

Become the Media

Nowadays, we can all be publishers and broadcasters, and we should be. Social media grants us platforms to publish or broadcast our own content. Setting up a blog, podcast, online or digital magazine, or online TV channel is so affordable that even teenagers and young children are getting in on the act.

What once required complex technology costing tens or hundreds of thousands of dollars has now been eclipsed by smart phones and apps. Internet celebrities are making their fortunes by endorsing products or services to their followers. And there's nothing stopping vegan business owners and entrepreneurs from doing the same. Many, such as Eco-Vegan Gal's Whitney Lauritsen and vegan image consultant Ginger Burr, are riding this new media wave and sharing the vegan message on their own channels, while making a living doing so.

Even Velez-Mitchell, who was the host of a major cable TV show for several years and a commentator on various high-profile shows before that, has moved away from mainstream and into independent broadcasting. In 2014, she launched

JaneUnchained.com, a multi-media publishing platform for stories related to crimes against people, animals, and the environment. "Go directly to people using social media. Get on Facebook, use blogs, Twitter, Instagram, Google Hangouts, YouTube, Pinterest, and so on," urges Velez-Mitchell.

How to Get Media Coverage

Whether you're looking to get into mainstream or independent media, it's all about stories. You need to find the right story at the right time and pitch it to the right journalist.

A journalist's job isn't to promote your business. That's what a PR person, also known as a publicist, does. A journalist's job is to produce great content that their audience will love, so that the audience keeps coming back. The more readers, viewers, or listeners, the better for the media outlet, as it allows them to sell advertising space or to sell their own or other people's products to their audience.

Journalists are looking for stories that inform, entertain, or inspire. If your story manages to crack all three, even better, but it must do at least one of those three.

Target the right media

It's your job to make journalists' jobs as easy as possible. Nowadays, journalists are overworked and understaffed, often doing the work of what previously would have been done by several journalists. They receive hundreds of pitches and press releases a day, so, to get noticed, you have to make it a no-brainer for them to say "yes" to you. This means coming up with relevant stories for their specific audience. A "spray and pray" approach, whereby you send out the same pitch and press release to hundreds of media outlets, is unlikely to get you results. Instead, make a list of the outlets you'd like to be featured in and—most importantly—the outlets that you know your target market consumes. Study them—their style and the type of content they run, then come up with relevant story ideas to pitch.

"At times, I've said to the health media, 'This is a healthy product.' I've said to the women's magazines, 'This is suitable for women of all ages.' I've said to the vegetarian media, 'This is vegetarian.' I've said to the organic media, 'It's organic,'" explains Karin Ridgers. "You don't need to hide that your product is vegan, but there are certain things that may be more key to playing the media game that's going to benefit your business. If your product is organic and you go to magazines that love organic stuff, really highlight that *and* say it's vegan. But if you go in and say, 'I'm vegan, I'm vegan, I'm vegan!' they're likely to say, 'So what?' It's the organic aspect that's relevant to their audience."

Start local

You may have thousands of followers on social media, and most of them likely come from across the globe or, at least, within your country. But if you're holding a local event or servicing your local area, your local media is a fast and easy way to get the word out. Local outlets are always looking for strong, quirky, interesting, entertaining stories with a local feel and you stand the best chance of getting in your local media than immediately appearing on *Ellen*.

Author and vegan lifestyle coach JL Fields regularly sends out press releases to her local media. While not every story gets covered, it lands her regular media, as well as writing opportunities. "I send out press releases and then I get an email from the editor of our local independent paper who says, 'Hey, we're doing our 2014 Things to Do in Colorado Springs. Can we hire you to write an article on what to do in Colorado Springs if you're a vegan?'" says Fields. "I send those press releases out and then the food editor of our very conservative daily newspaper quotes me when she's writing about ancient grains on why grains are important in a vegan diet. So those press releases often get me used as a resource and a source, and I now write a monthly vegan restaurant review for that very conservative daily newspaper. When I did my first cancer-prevention class, I sent out press releases, the newspaper did a huge story on it, and a local business journal also did a story on it. I keep being able to do my classes and I keep getting hired to do things because I let the local press know who I am, what I'm about and what I know. It's essential," says Fields.

Humane Wildlife Solutions's Kevin Newell has found local media to be a useful tool in growing his business. "We contacted local radio for our wildlife services and got a slot on the vet's show, which gave us free coverage to thousands of people. Getting your story in a local paper is always good too. We've found even years after the stories have been published, people will still remember you if you stand out enough," says Newell.

Nikki Medwell pulled off an outstanding feat by landing a recipe column in her local paper. It's remarkable because, as we learned in Chapter 4, Medwell's vegan bed and breakfast, Bed and Broccoli, is located in the heart of dairy country in Australia. "I run a Vegans in Shepparton Facebook page and somebody on that page said, 'Every Monday, the paper has this cooking column, and it's disgusting because it's always meat. Can you ask them to put some vegan food in?' We'd been interviewed several times by one of the journalists on the paper, and when I contacted her, she said it was perfect timing and gave me a column."

Fields, Newell, and Medwell are excellent examples of vegan business owners being proactive in contacting their local media, resulting in a win for everyone: their business, the media outlet, the media outlet's audience, and, of course, animals, as more people are exposed to vegan living.

Hooks
A hook is—like a clothes hanger—an angle on which to "hang" a story. It's a reason for a media outlet to publish or broadcast a particular story.

There are a multitude of media hooks. Here are a few examples:

Awards

Winning an award can be a good hook for a story for particular media. Sometimes, just being nominated can give your business exposure. One of the reasons Medwell has been interviewed several times by her local paper is because Bed and Broccoli won a local business award that resulted in a billboard campaign by the state government that garnered a lot of media interest.

Rubyfruit café owners Amanda Solomons and Simone Bateman have also benefited from local media by winning their local business awards on several occasions.

Depending on what your business is, you can also create your own awards.

Being quirky or "first"

This is where your USP comes in. If you're the first to market with a product or service (be sure to check that this really is the case), this is likely to attract the (right) media's attention. You may be the first in your local area (such as the first vegan café, or the first vegan Italian restaurant), in your nation, or in the world.

Tofurky, for example, received a ton of media when it first launched over 20 years ago because it was unique and innovative. More recently, Beyond Meat has been featured extensively in mainstream media, largely due to investment by Microsoft founder Bill Gates.

We saw earlier how local media love to feature local businesses with a good story. You can also use the fact that your products are made locally as a hook. "A lot of vegan products are home-grown. So, if you're a small business, sell yourself to the media as a mom and pop operation that's bringing something to the local economy," advises Velez-Mitchell.

Anniversary

While being first to market is a great way to get media coverage, what if your business is already established and no longer has that air of "new" about it? This is where the "anniversary" hook comes in. Journalists like to run stories around a particular milestone. Usually the longer the better, but sometimes as little as five or 10 years can give you an edge.

"As a mature brand that's been around for a while, we don't get as much press as some of the newer, sexier start-ups," says Tofurky's Seth Tibbott. "But in 2014, in the lead-up to Thanksgiving, we got considerable media interest because it was the 20th year for Tofurky, and Tofurky roast has been such an iconic product. It's still the number-one-selling meat alternative at Thanksgiving."

Tie into trends

What's "hot" right now? What topics are featuring endlessly in the media? At the time of writing, veganism and plant-based living are "on trend," so this is the perfect time to put yourself out there to the media.

"If you can package yourself as part of a massive trend, that's a great way to get media," says Velez-Mitchell. "Vegan eating is good for weight loss, health, and the environment, so that's three selling points. It's about timing, though, so maybe you put a pitch together for the holidays or after the Christmas holidays when people are trying to lose weight. A TV show will rarely cover a product unless it's particularly quirky; they cover issues. But they may have a guest to discuss an issue and that can correlate to your product if it helps people to lose weight, such as healthy snacks or raw vegan cheesecake."

As well as trends in society, also keep an eye on what the trends are in your industry, as this will give you ideas for stories.

A look on Twitter or Google Trends will tell you what topics are trending, again giving you fodder to come up with suitable media angles.

Be controversial

The media loves controversy and conflict, so being controversial can certainly help you to stand out and become a source for quotes. However, only do this if it comes from a genuine place. Don't do it just to get media attention. Only do it if you truly believe something and are willing to stand up and speak out about it.

"I get a lot of media coverage because I stand out by saying I'm against what the establishment is saying," says Cruelty Free Super's Lee Coates. "Because I'm so establishment and qualified in my industry, I can do that. I'll say what others in my industry won't say. I'm happy to talk about the things that are generally locked away in the cupboard in the hope that customers never find out, and the media loves that."

Collaborate

Teaming up with complementary businesses can work to your advantage in terms of gaining media coverage. We saw in Chapter 4 how some vegan business owners are collaborating to achieve a win-win.

JL Fields, for example, put out a press release to local media featuring her direct competition—other vegan lifestyle coaches. She focused on their particular specialities and the theme of the story was along the lines of how lucky the residents of Colorado Springs were because they had, not one, but four vegan lifestyle coaches—each with a particular focus—to choose from.

If your product is a healthy vegan one, you could team up with a vegan nutritionist or other healthcare practitioner to put together a joint pitch or media release.

Celebrities

Like it or not, we live in a celebrity-obsessed culture. The majority of people are followers, not leaders, so are happy to buy what their favorite celebrities promote. If you can get your vegan product or service in front of a celebrity and they agree to endorse it, it's an easy angle to get media interest. It doesn't need to be an A-lister; a popular reality TV star can suffice.

"If you get a celebrity to say, 'I love this product,' it raises your profile, it raises awareness, and you can promote the endorsement," says Karin Ridgers. "I don't think anything beats that to really raise your profile and to be seen as that go-to person in your industry."

Vegan acupuncturist Heather Lounsbury from Live Natural Live Well is savvy when it comes to approaching and securing celebrity endorsements for her healthcare business. "When I first started out, I cold-called, and sent out letters and then emails to managers of every major musician and actor you can think of, and I followed up with all of them. I was so tenacious. I was like, 'I'm reaching out to Paul McCartney's manager; I don't care!'" she laughs. "I didn't get Paul as a client, but I did get other pretty amazing artists as patients of mine."

Lounsbury also places gift certificates for her services in celebrity showbags at major events, such as the Academy Awards or Emmy Awards. "They give gift bags to all the celebrities who are nominated and win, as well as the presenters, so it's fantastic exposure," she says.

When Nichole Dandrea launched her Nicobella range of chocolates, she was able to get them in front of actor and author Alicia Silverstone, who wrote a blog post about them. "Partnering with successful people like that is a brilliant way to gain exposure," says Dandrea.

Over in Australia, Jessica Bailey of The Cruelty Free Shop secured a pictorial feature in the *Daily Mail* in a story about US vegan actor Pamela Anderson giving an assortment basket from the shop to Australian TV personality Lara Bingle. Not only did The Cruelty Free Shop win, so too did all the brands featured in the assortment basket—another example of successful collaboration with like-minded businesses.

The above are a few hooks you can use to start to come up with ideas to secure media coverage for your vegan business.

For a free list of 55 media angles for vegan business owners—go to **www.veganbusinessmedia.com/angles**

Respond to journalists' callouts

In addition to coming up with ideas for stories, another way to get media coverage is to respond to requests by journalists who are already working on a story and are looking for an expert to provide comment.

Some journalists put their callouts on Twitter, so it's a good idea to follow the key journalists, bloggers, vloggers, podcasters, producers, and presenters for your target outlets on social media. This has the added benefit of allowing you to keep up to date with what they're working on and to build rapport with them by engaging in discussions or retweeting their tweets.

There are also services you can sign up for to receive callouts from journalists. The two main platforms are HARO (Help a Reporter Out) and SourceBottle.

SourceBottle began in Australia but also now services the US and UK, while HARO is focused predominantly on the US market.

Both these platforms are free to register as an expert source, and I highly encourage you to subscribe to them. The way they work is you sign up to receive queries (also known as callouts) about your area of expertise and they land in your email inbox several times a day. With HARO, you can sign up to the main list as well as category-specific lists. With SourceBottle, you can specify keywords that are related to your area of expertise.

For example, if you're a vegan shoe brand, you might list 'fashion' as one of your keywords and receive queries from journalists working on fashion-related stories. If you're a health practitioner, you might list 'weight loss' or 'natural foods' or 'healthy eating' as your keywords and receive queries related to those topics.

The thing is, journalists receive a lot of queries, so here's how to boost your chances of being picked:

Research the media outlet (quickly)

HARO and SourceBottle both have an option for the journalist to remain anonymous. On SourceBottle you may see generic 'national women's magazine' or 'weekly podcast' and only find out the name of the outlet if and when you get a response.

If the name of the media outlet is included, do a quick bit of research to ascertain if it's a good fit for you. There's another difference between HARO and SourceBottle in that SourceBottle allows small, independent media such as bloggers and podcasters to seek expert sources for quotes and for guest blog writers, but HARO doesn't.

You need to decide how valuable a particular media outlet is to you and if it's worth your time and energy to respond to a callout. If it's a brand new blog or podcast with little reach, it may not be in your best interest to respond.

On the other hand, many small blogs or podcasts grow to have large audiences and if you've proved helpful in the beginning, the journalist is more likely to include you again as a trusted and reliable source. Your call.

Don't spend ages checking out the media outlet because you also need to:

Respond FAST (while still being accurate)

The quicker you are to respond to a journalist's query on SourceBottle or HARO, the more likely you are to get their attention. Because they receive so many responses, they often run out of energy after combing through the first 20 or so. If they're on a super tight deadline, they won't even read that many. So get in quick.

Be succinct (but don't cut corners)

Don't send long, rambling responses. Journalists don't have time to read an essay. Keep your response succinct, but not too short. By this I mean use full sentences rather than three-word answers to queries, so the journalist can quote you without needing to contact you.

Bullet points can be a good idea, especially if the journalist is requesting tips. Some magazine journalists are seeking tips in a short list format for sidebars to accompany the main editorial feature. It depends on the nature of the query, which brings us to the next point:

Respond precisely (follow the brief)

In 17 years working as a journalist for a range of media, I still find it exasperating that many people (including publicists—some at major PR firms!) seem unable to follow simple instructions when responding to my requests for sources, quotes, or contributors.

Make sure you read the callout and determine exactly what the journalist is after. Don't just scan it, see a particular keyword and then fire off a one-size-fits-all response that doesn't address the specific requirements of the query.

If the callout asks for five short tips on the latest trends in healthy eating, include those five tips in your response. Don't send the journalist to your website or an article you've written elsewhere on the internet. They don't have time to search through and look for the information. Make their job easy and put the information they request, in the format they request, right in front of them.

If the query is looking for organic brands and yours is not, don't waste the journalist's (or your) time by responding. Only respond to callouts that are a match to what the journalist is looking for.

Do NOT pitch other ideas to the journalist. This is against the terms of service for these platforms and it's bad practice. If you're tempted to say, 'I know you're looking for X, but how about Y instead?' don't do it. Your response will be deleted and you'll be listed as an unreliable annoyance in the journalist's mind, which can ruin your chances of future coverage.

Demonstrate your (relevant) expertise

A journalist needs to know that you're qualified to make a comment or be a featured guest on TV or radio. To build their trust, you need to demonstrate your credentials. If you have several areas of expertise, focus on what's required for the query. For example, if you're a marketer and the query is in regards to social media, show your expertise in social media marketing when responding.

If you've won an award that's relevant to the subject of the callout, include that. If you've authored a book on the topic, mention that up front. Don't be afraid to 'sell' yourself. The journalist is looking for a credible expert—it's your job to establish yourself as that. This isn't the time to be modest.

That said, only respond to queries where you DO have the expertise required.

Make it easy for journalists to contact you

Include your full signature at the end of your query: name, title, email address, physical address, phone number, and website URL. If you're chosen to be featured, the journalist needs this information on hand if they want to interview you. Even if they don't need to interview you because they're going to use the quotes you provided in your response, you want to make sure your name and title appear correctly in the story and make it easy for the journalist to follow up and check anything.

Check your response before sending

Even though you need to respond fast, you still need to edit your response to make sure it's free of spelling mistakes or typos. The cleaner your copy, the easier the journalist's job, which puts you ahead of other people whose responses contain errors.

Don't give up (keep responding)

It can be disheartening to send responses to callouts and not receive a reply. Generally, you'll only get a reply if you're being considered for an interview or your quotes are to be used. Keep responding. Not only is it good practice and you'll get faster and better with experience but also it can result in other editorial opportunities down the track.

As Nicole Fallon, assistant editor at *Business News Daily*, says in her *LinkedIn Pulse* article:

"Due to space and time constraints, I'm simply not able to feature every source who answers my query, even if they fit all the criteria I look for. But sometimes I will add a particularly good HARO respondent to my source list and make a note to reach out in the future if I'm writing about that topic again." (Fallon, 2014, para. 10)

I see far too few vegan businesses responding to journalists' queries on HARO or SourceBottle, even when the callout is a perfect fit to gain media exposure. So, bear these tips in mind and start responding!

Visit **www.sourcebottle.com** and **www.helpareporter.com** to get started.

PR Firms

Depending on your budget, you can do your own PR, or, as you grow, you may want to hire a professional. There are pros and cons. Even if you hire a PR person, it's good to learn how to do your own and to know the pitfalls and questions to ask. You can also be prepared and be proactive in recognizing and coming up with suitable angles that the PR firm can then pitch. If you do hire a PR firm, try to work with a media coach as well to gain maximum benefits.

When to hire a PR firm

When should you hire a professional publicist? According to Evo-lotus PR's Kezia Jauron, it depends on your industry and focus of your business. "I will say that you only have one chance to launch a new company or new product, so doing it poorly at the outset makes it more difficult for you down the road. Reviewers are really only interested in your new restaurant when it first opens, and perhaps when there's been a very significant change, like a new chef or new location," says Jauron. "However, in a sort of media paradox, journalists are often risk-averse, and don't want to give ink to something or someone unproven. If you're a personal trainer, you're going to need a few customer references in order for a journalist to take you seriously, and that might be tough when you're just starting out."

What to consider when hiring a PR firm

"Recently, I've had three people come to me who have been let down by PR companies, and was shocked by what I heard," says Mad Promotions' Karin Ridgers, who's frustrated with some large players in the PR industry leaving their clients disappointed. "It's just absolutely crazy. They don't care about you or your business; they're paid to promote anyone and everyone. You'll meet the account manager, who's all lovely and experienced. You'll have a glass of wine, and it all sounds fantastic; however, they're not going to be doing your promotion. They'll put a teenage intern with little or no experience on your project, but charge you a lot of money. I have low-paid interns calling me, asking for my help because they're out of their depth."

This is the negative face of PR, and it's why you must be judicious when choosing a PR firm to represent you. "You must do your research," warns Ridgers. "Talk to other people about their experiences working with that firm. Is the PR person on the same wavelength? Do they really care about you? I had one business owner come to me and say, 'I employed a PR company and they didn't even know what vegan was.' And I'm like, 'They don't even know what vegan is? Your whole brand is vegan—why on earth did you work with them?'"

Main Street Vegan Academy director and author Victoria Moran, who has appeared on *The Oprah Winfrey Show* twice in relation to her spiritual and self-help books, advises using high-end PR companies that are well connected to key journalists, editors, and producers, particularly if your goal is to be featured in major national or international, high-profile media outlets. "Too often, people will try to fit PR into their budget—and I've done this too—and they'll get a lower-level PR firm that they can afford. The people are lovely and they work hard, but they don't have these connections, and you end up paying for something you could be doing yourself. So, if you're going to spend your money on PR, look for somebody who goes to lunch with the producers and the editors you want to reach. If it's out of your price range, you may be able to do extremely creative campaigns on your own and online for now, and create a PR fund for some major project you'll do later," says Moran.

Beware of publicists at independent publishing houses because the quality varies. I've received some shocking pitches and media releases that are guaranteed only one action: the pressing of the delete key! One, in particular, addressed their salutation to 'Dear Press, Book Sellers, and Book Lovers.' If you're using a small, independent publishing house to produce your book, ask them to explain their media strategy in detail to you, including samples of media releases and pitches they've used with other authors. Or, do the PR yourself.

Expectations and guarantees
When hiring a media coach to teach you how to do your own PR, or hiring a PR firm, there are no guarantees of media coverage.

"The PR person has to manage the expectations, and what I say to people is that there's no guarantee with PR. I don't know what the editor is going to say or what the radio producer is going to say or what the celebrity is going to say," says Ridgers.

Jauron agrees. "There really are no guarantees. I can't make a reporter cover your story. Lack of results does not necessarily mean lack of effort. It can simply mean lack of interest on the part of media contacts. It's demoralizing for everyone when, despite our best efforts, we can't get attention for a particular story."

While every effort may not be a success, it's important to keep trying and pitching media regularly. As we've seen earlier, it's important to select the right PR firm. Equally important is what the PR firm needs from you, and a diligent company will vet you before taking you on as a client.

Jauron tells prospective clients that a PR campaign requires a major commitment from them. "They're going to have to work hard, be communicative, responsive to me, and deliver what they've promised. They have to invest not just money but also significant time and effort. It isn't a one-way street where they hire a PR person and everything is handled. They may have to do much more work than they expect, and they can't drop the ball.

"We also turn down opportunities when the contact person seems difficult to work with, unprofessional, or unreliable. People get off on the wrong foot with me when they don't keep an appointment we've set for a phone call or are unreasonably late. Also, I can't have clients who flake on an interview with a journalist. That journalist may never work with me again, and I don't want to risk that happening. I also expect full disclosure. Clients and prospective clients need to be completely honest with us about their business situation and their future plans. If anything is withheld, it can be very detrimental down the line," says Jauron.

Ridgers has similar criteria. "I look for someone who's passionate, likable, and fun. I look for someone who's going to take PR seriously, who will reply to my emails, and understand that if I ask a question, I need the answer urgently because a magazine editor's probably asking me to ask it," she says.

PR Mistakes

Too promotional
As noted earlier, journalists aren't there to promote your business.

Their job is to run stories that inform, entertain, or inspire their audiences. It's up to you to find the stories in your business.

Cut out hyperbole. Journalists are trained to spot BS. Using terms such as *world-leading* or, as one author put in a media release to me, describing his book, "*The greatest gift to human-kind,*" isn't the best move.

"The biggest mistake unseasoned people tend to make when trying to get media attention is being too overtly promotional. Talking to a journalist isn't the same as selling to a customer," says Jauron.

Too demanding

It's tempting when you're passionate about your product or service to contact journalists with a story and tell them they "must" or "should" cover it. Don't do this. No one likes to be told what they must or should do, and journalists are no exception. Watch your language.

"I've seen some presumptuous behavior from business owners. Keep in mind, you're not entitled to attention—you have to work for it and earn it by having a good story to tell," says Jauron.

Waffling on

Remember, your number one job is to make a journalist's job as easy as possible. Remember also that most journalists are overworked, underpaid, and understaffed. So, sending them long, rambling emails isn't helpful. Be succinct and make sure you provide everything a journalist needs at their fingertips.

"In TV, you've got to have video because we need to see what you look and sound like," says Jane Velez-Mitchell. "People get picked to be spokespeople on TV for different reasons: how much energy they have, what they look like, or how they sound. So have a great pitch reel and provide a link in your email message so the media can see it. I used to get pitches from lawyers to come on my show, and it helped to provide me with a photo and link to them speaking. Do it succinctly and use bullet points, a great headline, and photos."

Spelling errors and typos
While you don't need to be a great writer, because it's the journalist's job to put together the story, sending a pitch or press release full of spelling mistakes and typos doesn't give journalists a lot of faith in your expertise or credentials. Rightly or wrongly, it gives the impression that your information may not be accurate. If it's not your strong point, get someone with editing or proof-reading skills to check your email and release before sending it.

Create a Media Room and Online Media Kit
A media room is a dedicated page or section on your website for journalists to find and download helpful information about you and your business. In addition to containing all your press releases, it should also include an **online and downloadable media kit** (also known as a press kit).

A media kit is a "brochure" that gives reporters and producers useful information about you that they'll use when deciding whether or not to feature you in their program or publication. In the past, a media kit was a full-color physical brochure that was mailed to media outlets. Nowadays, you get to save money and trees by making it available on your website.

It's important to have your media kit in two formats:
• Text and images on the web pages
• A downloadable PDF

This gives journalists the option of scrolling through online, as well as printing out your media kit or saving it and forwarding it to other members of their editorial team. Again, I'll stress, it's up to you to make the journalist's job as easy as possible.

What should you include in your online media kit?

The following are a list of things to include in your online media kit—regardless of how much or little media experience you've had:

A dynamic bio

So many professional bios are boring and bland. Instead of sending a journalist to sleep with your bio, you want to entice and excite them. Sure, you need to put in the key essential information about you, but also include the quirky stuff that makes you different.

For example, in the "About" page on my website at **www.katrinafox.com**, I've got a section called "7 things you may not know about me." This is gold for journalists. Yes, we want to know you're an expert with solid credentials—that's taken as read. But what makes you stand out and maximize your chances of being featured is that difference. So, if you've done something amazing or have an unusual hobby (a legal one!), even if it has nothing to with your expertise, include it anyway because it makes you interesting.

Make sure you include your bio in different lengths: short, medium, and long. You can even include a tweetable 140-character bio as well as a two-sentence summary that can be used at the bottom of opinion pieces or articles you write for the media.

It's far better that you provide journalists with this information, because it saves them time, so they'll feel warm and fuzzy toward you, but also because you get to control how you're positioned.

If your business is a small to medium enterprise or corporation, include (dynamic) bios of key staff members.

Facts related to your expertise

Offer findings and statistics to emphasize the importance of your field and how those facts are newsworthy.

Journalists love statistics and because we're so busy nowadays, the more information and research you can provide us with, the more we'll appreciate you as a helpful, valuable and reliable source.

About your business

This is different than your bio or those of your staff. In this section, you want to present information about the business itself, such as:

- How it started
- How long it's been in operation
- Why it was founded
- Its mission statement
- What it does
- The main products and services
- Its point of difference

When journalists are in the planning stages of a story, they do background research on you and your business. Yes, they'll Google you, but by providing key data in your online media kit, you save them time and have a greater influence over what information appears about your brand.

Photos of you

I encourage you, if you haven't already done so, to invest in a professional photo shoot. Make sure you get a decent headshot, as well as some standing and three-quarter-length images.

You can also include in your media kit some non-professional character shots, although these must still be of good quality, but they must be in addition to, not a substitute for, professional photos.

Images are particularly important for TV, as it's a visual medium, and a standout photo can also increase your chances of being featured in print. Sometimes, there's not room for a long story, but a picture and caption can bring you just as many leads.

Make sure your images are high resolution for journalists to download. Digital images are packed with pixels and the more there are, the better the image will look when it's enlarged. This is particularly pertinent when it comes to print publications. Resolution should be at least 300 dpi (dots per inch) for print. The last thing you want is the designer to blow up your image to take up a whole page or to feature you on the cover, and the image "pixelates"—that is, it becomes grainy.

For the web, lower-resolution images can suffice, but, to be on the safe side, always offer the option to download high-resolution images.

Product photos

If you sell products and can come up with interesting stories around them, make sure you have photos of the products. Use the same guidelines for the photos of you for product photos: high-resolution, great quality.

Have the products photographed by a professional who is experienced in this field as they can position them to reflect your brand. If you sell a high-end, luxury product, the last thing you want is for it to come across as cheap and tacky because you snapped it with your phone camera!

Professional photographers can also ensure your products are taken in the right light and at particular angles to make them interesting for the media. Journalists don't like bland, boring imagery—of you or your products.

Client list

Mention clients that you've worked with. The more well-known they are, the better.

This gives you credibility in the eyes of reporters—as well as the public—that you're an expert in your field. TV and radio producers in particular want to make sure they book guests who know their stuff. Listing big-name clients or a long list of clients reassures them that you know what you're talking about.

Include the logos of the companies you've worked for to

break up lots of text in the media kit.

Testimonials

Featuring endorsements again positions you as an expert, providing 'social proof'. Remember, we put more faith in what others say about us, over what we say about ourselves.

If you have any high-profile or celebrity endorsements of your products or services, feature these prominently as—rightly or wrongly—it provides journalists with an additional point of interest.

Frequently asked questions (FAQs)

Offering a list of frequently asked questions can help address what reporters and clients want to ask about in addition to their concerns, without wasting time exchanging emails. Remember, you want to make journalists' jobs as easy as possible!

This also helps you to formulate your responses so you can be comfortable with them if you get asked them in interviews, particularly on radio and TV when the pressure can be high.

Story ideas

Listing story ideas in your field of expertise can give reporters subject matter to cover that they may not have thought of, or provide them with additional angles on a current story, which can result in extra coverage for you.

Journalists, particularly those working in niche or specialist media, are often looking for stories, and by doing some of the legwork for them, you're more likely to get coverage.

Come up with a list of 'evergreen' story ideas: these are ideas that are not time-sensitive and can be run at anytime. Tips or 'How to' guides are examples of evergreen angles.

Press releases

Have a section in your online media room for your press releases (also called media releases). They need to be all in one place for journalists to access. You can either write these as blog posts and provide a list of links to them under the heading of 'Media releases', or you can hotlink the title of each one to open as a PDF.

Clips and logos from previous media experience

If you've been featured in any kind of media, don't be shy about it! Put those clips in your media kit with links. Radio and TV producers will often look at these to see how you come across before booking you as a guest.

Also include the media logos of the outlets you've appeared in with the text "As featured on" or "As seen in." This gives you massive credibility, not only to the media, but also your customers. It tells journalists that you know what you're doing and that they can trust you to offer a great quote or be a charismatic guest.

If you haven't had any media experience, put a link to your own media channel, such as YouTube or your blog.

Contact information

Don't force journalists to search through your website looking for your contact information. Even if you have a separate Contact menu (which I recommend you do), still include your full contact details in your online media room.

Tip: **Do NOT have a Contact *Form* in your online media room**. Most journalists won't take the time to fill it out. If they're on deadline, they need to be able to get in touch with you, or your publicist if you have one, immediately.

Provide a **phone number (landline and mobile), email address and physical address** (journalists are unlikely to write to you, but it helps to know where you're located in terms of city, state and country).

Include your website URL (even though the journalist is on your site, make it easy for them to cut and paste your contact information).

Also **include links to your social media channels**. Nowadays, journalists will check these out and it offers you an extra opportunity to showcase your expertise. If you have a large following and plenty of interaction on these platforms, it again demonstrates your credibility.

Remember, put all this information on individual web pages that are clearly labelled and ensure they are easy to navigate. The more professional your media kit, the more you increase your chances of being featured in the media. Also include the information as a downloadable PDF. You can hire a designer at a reasonable rate to make your media kit look snazzy.

What About Paid Ads?
Some media coaches or PR firms will tell you to steer clear of paid adverts and to only try for editorial coverage. I don't necessarily agree. Sometimes, paid ads can serve a purpose, but, as with all marketing, you need to test and measure. With print, it can be hard to measure your return on investment, but, if it's a highly specific, targeted media outlet, an ad can be useful, if not to get sales, then to raise awareness of your brand. Online advertising is easier to measure, as you can track how many people are visiting your site from the advert.

Some print or online magazines will give editorial to advertisers as part of a deal. It's a touchy subject and one that many journalists find irritating and unethical. But the nature of journalism is changing. Also for free media, whose only form of income is advertising, this practice is common.

Native advertising is becoming more popular and frequent. As we saw in Chapter 5, this is a piece of content created to showcase a brand but created in such a way that it appears like other editorial content. It doesn't look like an advert. Many mainstream and large independent media include native advertising on their websites. If you scroll to the end of a story, and you see a section titled "Recommended" or "Other Stories You May Like" or similar, much of this content is paid native advertising.

Whenever possible, aim to get "free" publicity through being featured in a story in the media because of the benefits outlined at the beginning of this chapter. Too many vegan business owners shy away from putting together a PR strategy—either on their own or with a media coach or PR firm. But if we truly want to make veganism mainstream, while growing our businesses, PR isn't an option, it's a necessity.

Chapter 10
Other Ways to Market Your Business

Take a Booth or Stall at a Festival, Expo or Other Event

Social media and online marketing may be all the rage, but there are plenty of benefits to getting in front of potential customers up close and personal.

More than 71,000 people attended the 35th annual Natural Products Expo West in early 2015—a 7.2 percent increase from the previous year. The natural, organic, and healthy products event took over the entire Anaheim Center in California.

On the other side of the pond, VegFestUK also continues to see higher numbers pass through its vegan lifestyle festivals across the UK each year. After two successful stints at the prestigious Olympia in 2013 and 2014, attracting over 9,000 visitors on each occasion, VegfestUK London moved into the venue's largest exhibition area in October 2015.

Events like this offer a great opportunity to get your products or services in front of people. As well as meeting your existing and potential customers, if you sell a physical product, it's a chance to allow them to taste, touch, or try on your wares.

"When you're first starting out, doing events and festivals is a brilliant way to build your brand awareness," says Addiction Food's Grant Campbell. "People can literally taste our products and get to know us. Over time, we've become known in the vegan community, so having a stall at, for example, the Sydney Vegan Expo or Cruelty Free Festival, allows us to maintain our brand presence and continue to connect with our customers."

Vx's Rudy Penando agrees. "Our most successful marketing effort is direct promotion at festivals," he says.

Whether you're at a specifically vegan or vegetarian event or not, taking a booth or stall is an opportunity to make sales on the day to cover your costs or even turn a profit. This may not be the case for service providers, such as healthcare practitioners, for example, where the focus is more likely to be on meet and greet and getting interested parties to sign up to receive information from you after the event. Festivals and expos tend to favor small goods, particularly food, clothing, and bric-a-brac in terms of numbers of sales made on the day.

Offering show specials is a good way to both drive sales and get as many people as possible to try your products. Yaoh hemp products owner Tim Barford employs these strategies, such as a 'Buy one, get one free' at the VegFestUK and other events he organizes throughout the year.

In addition to meeting your existing and potential customers, taking a booth or stall at a festival, expo, or other event is a great way to connect with other business owners, particularly socially conscious ones. "We enjoy meeting other stallholders at Sydney Vegan Expo to discuss current challenges, solutions, and new innovations happening within the vegan movement and industry," says Addiction Food's Grant Campbell.

As well as the many veg and vegan events, look for opportunities at events that focus on sustainable living and natural health. Depending on what your product or service is, local street fairs, music or arts festivals, trade shows, or corporate expos may be relevant.

You can even run your own event, as The Cruelty Free Shop's Jessica Bailey does on a regular basis. Bailey holds wine and cheese tastings and book launches at her stores, as well as hosting her annual Vegan Day Out event in Sydney and Melbourne.

Tips for exhibiting
1. Make a list of events where you know your target market will likely attend.
2. If the event has been held before, talk to previous

stallholders and find out what their experience was like (most events list past exhibitors on their website, but if they don't, ask the organizers for a list).

3. Have a clear aim of what you want to achieve by exhibiting at each event.

4. Work out your costs in detail to determine the viability of exhibiting—remember to include things like fuel, parking, permits, insurance, signage and promotional material.

5. Depending on your budget and where you're at in your business, decide whether sponsoring an event may be worth your while. Being associated with a well-regarded and well-promoted event can boost your brand's reputation as well as your profile.

6. Have fun while learning a lot!

This article by Jennifer Pardoe of Zest Plant Based Food Consulting offers some handy tips for food producers on how to exhibit successfully at events: **www.veganbusinessmedia.com/ are-you-damaging-your-vegan-brand-by-making-these-mistakes-at-food-shows**

Word of Mouth
A recommendation from a friend, family member, or work colleague can beat award-winning sales or marketing copy. A glowing testimonial from someone we like and trust for your product or service will far more likely lead to us to buying from you.

Of course, the reverse is also true. You may be all set to buy a product or service when a friend advises you not to. All of a sudden, your mind is filled with doubt, and, to be on the safe side, you don't buy.

As a business owner, you want to cultivate what marketing guru Seth Godin calls "sneezers." These are people who love your product and take every opportunity to broadcast that fact.

They're your raving fans who'll tell anyone who'll listen how fantastic your product or service is. These people are gold. Treat them well, for they'll be a key factor in the success of your business.

Truth Belts owner Renia Pruchnicki attracts sales on some of her higher-priced belts due to word-of-mouth referrals. "I came across a technique of making some of my belts with recycled car tires. They're incredible quality and people see that. I sell them for around $68 Canadian dollars, and a lot of those sales come from people telling their friends," says Pruchnicki.

The "steady flow" of customers at Bed and Broccoli all comes from word-of-mouth promotions, according to owner Nikki Medwell, and this includes social media. As Veggie Grill's T.K. Pillan noted in Chapter 8, social media is an amplification of word of mouth.

Free Stuff

Free giveaways can be an opportunity for people to try your product or service. But be careful how you go about this and what you offer. If you're a food business, it's worth allocating a portion of your marketing budget to free samples, particularly at a festival, expo, or event.

Nicobella's Nichole Dandrea stresses the importance of offering free samples at shows. "If we don't demo the product, people don't try it. They aren't just going to pick up a bag of chocolates that they haven't heard of before, especially since they're at a higher price point, and make that investment when they don't know what it tastes like," says Dandrea.

Bounty Burgers's Loren Lembke agrees. "My best sales reps are my samples," she says.

But if you're a service provider who works by the hour, offering free sessions can be a time suck and even devalue the worth of your services. Instead, you could offer a free digital download, such as an ebook, audio or video file—something you create once that can be delivered endlessly and with no shipping costs.

Healthcare practitioners Clare Mann and Tracie O'Keefe offer a number of free "tasters" for potential clients to experience them as therapists/coaches. Mann offers a short audio program on how to overcome stress and anxiety, while O'Keefe gives away a complimentary deep relaxation hypnosis MP3 file. In addition, both create regular videos for their YouTube channels, along with blog posts on their websites.

Offering these kinds of giveaways from your website is a great way to encourage people to sign up to your database so you can email them periodically. The downloadable item—known as a lead magnet—can be set up to automatically be delivered to the subscriber, saving you a lot of time.

Speaking, Presenting, and Training

In addition to creating audio and video on your social media channels and website, speaking, presenting, and training are important tools in your marketing inventory. As a speaker/trainer, you have the opportunity to position yourself as the authority in your field. Whether you're inspiring your audience with your presentation, or teaching them practical skills, you're showcasing your expertise, which can help you build rapport and trust. This is important because people buy from those they like and trust.

Main Street Vegan Academy's Victoria Moran is an experienced motivational speaker who was regularly hired by the corporate sector for many years. Nowadays, she dazzles audiences at veg, vegan, and health events with her passion for and depth of knowledge on vegan living. This attracts clients who resonate with her style and personality to sign up for her coach training program, without any need for a "hard sell."

Author and vegan lifestyle coach JL Fields runs cooking classes as a way to gain clients. "I don't necessarily make a whole lot of money from the classes themselves, but people hire me as a coach, so I look at my classes as a marketing tool to then do that individual lifestyle work with people. I don't charge a lot of money for the classes, but I give a lot of value and content, and that inspires people to want to hire me to work with them individually," says Fields.

222 Veggie Vegan's Ben Asamani took a similar approach in the early days of the restaurant by offering free cooking classes to encourage people to come through the doors. "I remember when I started to fit out the premises, a guy passed by and asked me what business I was opening, and I told him I was going to open a vegetarian restaurant. The guy laughed and said, 'You must be joking.' So, in the beginning, I gave lessons to people about how to create a healthy lifestyle. This got them to come into the restaurant," says Asamani.

While it's a good idea to learn some speaking, presentation, and training skills, the most important considerations are your passion, combined with your expertise in your subject. Passion is particularly important, because we've all, no doubt, experienced deathly boring slideshow presentations by well-meaning experts. An imperfect, yet passionate and enthusiastic presentation will resonate more with your audience than a slick but dispassionate one. Consider joining a speakers' association such as National Speakers Association or Toastmasters International (both have branches in various cities across the globe) to pick up some tips and network with other speakers.

The more you speak, the better you'll get, so do it regularly. Check out business and other networking events in your local area, as they're often looking for speakers on a range of topics. And, of course, run your own events.

Webinars
Webinars are a great way to reach larger audiences. Since they're online, people from different geographical locations can take part. There are several platforms available to host a webinar, from stalwarts such as GoToWebinar (monthly costs may be

prohibitive) to newer and more affordable technologies that connect with Google Hangouts.

You can use a mix of video, audio, and slide presentations to engage and deliver content to participants, who can use a chat box to ask questions or provide feedback. Webinars can be offered free or paid, and many of the platforms come with snazzy-looking landing pages where people can register. These can be synchronized to your email marketing list provider so you can continue to market to these people (with their permission of course—which we'll cover in the section on email marketing).

Books

Becoming an author is a great way to boost your credibility and generate opportunities for you and your business. "Books are what have helped me catapult my business, in the sense that it has given me street cred," says JL Fields, who picked up her first book deal after attending the Vida Vegan Con media and blogging conference in the US. Fields met author and registered dietician Ginny Messina, who asked her a few months later, to collaborate on the book *Vegan for Her* by writing the chapter on ethical veganism and the cookbook section. Messina chose Fields for the project after seeing her website.

"I told Ginny I'm not a trained chef and that I don't even take pretty pictures of food. And she said, 'That's why I want you. Your recipes are good; they're wholesome, decadent on occasion. And what I want is for people to pick up this book and think they can cook this way,'" explains Fields. "So I was rewarded for just writing simple, home-cooked recipes with not very fancy photos."

A year later, Fields received an email from a publishing house, wanting to commission her to write a book called *Vegan Pressure Cooking*, also after having reviewed her website. "I'm consistently being truthful about what I know," says Fields. "I became obsessed with my pressure cooker! I think it's the coolest thing in the world, and then I got a book deal from that, and now, I get asked to do cooking demos, and I get invited to veg fests. And when I go to a veg fest, I often meet a vendor who owns a company, and they ask me to do some work for them."

Live Natural Live Well's Heather Lounsbury raised her expert status even more by writing a book, *Fix Your Mood with Food*; Sharon Gannon's books help to cement her credibility in the yoga world and raise the profile of the Jivamukti school; Victoria Moran's vegan lifestyle books raise awareness of her various Main Street Vegan projects; Tracie O'Keefe and Clare Mann use books to position themselves as mindset and health experts; and Candle Cafe's Joy Pierson's books keep the iconic restaurant chain top of mind for organic, vegan fine dining worldwide.

It's important to note, you're unlikely to make your fortune from book sales alone. Unless you're in the same league as JK Rowling, the numbers of books sold won't be enough to generate significant regular income. Instead, see books as a marketing tool to present you with other opportunities—such as speaking, training, and consulting—that attract higher fees.

Nowadays, you can have complete control over your book if you choose to self-publish. Self-publishing is no longer the last resort it may once have been, and, in many cases, is the better option. Some self-published authors' books outsell those put out by traditional publishers, who are often very reluctant to publish books by first-time authors.

Having been published by two mainstream publishers, as well as self-publishing, I'm familiar with the pros and cons of both.

Traditional publishers
If you're offered a book deal, the advantages are that the publisher bears the costs of editing and production. You may even be offered a commission up front, plus royalties from the sale of each book.

In some circles, being published by a mainstream publisher is perceived to give you a certain kudos.

Traditional publishers also tend to have established relationships with distributors, which can increase your chances of being picked up by bookstores.

The downside to signing a contract with a publisher is that, to some extent, you lose control of your book. While good publishers work with their authors, at the end of the day, they have the final say on how your book ends up, including the cover design and title.

Also, while they may send you a marketing survey to complete, be aware that most traditional publishers will expect you to do a lot of your own marketing and PR nowadays.

Self-publishing
The main advantage of self-publishing is you retain control over your title—everything from the content to the cover design. This means you can include references (and, in the ebook version, hotlinks) to your products and services in the book; you can even include adverts at the back from sponsors or partners.

The downside to self-publishing is you bear the costs of editing and production. You may think that you'll save money by hiring a cheap editor, but what you get will be so full of errors they didn't catch that you'll have to shell out more money for a second edit. Make sure you ask potential editors to do a sample edit, provide references, and tell you their process and how many edit passes they'll do.

Getting a distributor for your self-published book can be more difficult, but is by no means impossible.

Production costs can be expensive for print books, although print on demand (a book is printed only when a sale has been made) has made it a much more affordable process.

Ebooks
With more and more people reading books electronically, ebooks have increased in popularity. They're inexpensive to produce, and anyone can take advantage of Amazon's Kindle Direct

Publishing platform to format, upload, and sell their books. That said, if you do have a budget for a print book, I recommend producing both, as not everyone has access to a computer, Kindle, or other ereading device. Also, a print book is a tangible item that works well for in-person marketing opportunities, such as live events. You can self-publish inexpensive print books to give away like business cards, and people are far more likely to read them, keep them, and remember you.

Book signings and author tours
Holding a book signing or launch offers people the chance to meet you in person and, again, positions you as the expert. Consider teaming up with a local bookstore, vegan store, or festival organizer to create a joint event that's a win for everyone—the festival or store gets more customers, who will likely buy other products, and you don't have to pay for expensive venue hire.

Email Marketing
Every business owner needs to do this. Even if you're a social media superstar, you must have your own database of people who you can contact directly. As we noted in Chapter 8, a social media platform may terminate its service, or even just your account, leaving you in the lurch. Remember, there have been instances of business or fan pages on Facebook, for example, with hundreds of thousands of followers, being closed down. If those people are also on your email database, it's not such a disaster.

Email marketing service providers
An email marketing service provider isn't the same as an email or internet service provider. You do *not* want to be manually sending emails to people through your Outlook, Gmail, Yahoo or other email accounts and CCing or BCCing people in on them. For one, it's against most anti-spam laws, and, it's inefficient.

Instead, you need an email marketing service. There are

many available for different budgets. MailChimp was the most popular among interviewees for this book. It offers a free service as well as a paid service. At the other end of the scale is Infusionsoft, an all-in-one customer relationship management system that combines sophisticated email marketing, along with the ability to keep detailed notes of clients who are tagged according to their various actions. It also offers a shopping cart, your own affiliate program, and more. There are several others in the mid-range market.

Do NOT sign people up to your email list without their permission. This is also against most anti-spam laws and if you continually violate them, your email marketing service provider can shut you down. Even if someone gives you their business card, or you've exchanged emails with them, this doesn't constitute permission for you to sign them up to your list. It's far better to ask if they'd like to receive information from you. If they buy a product from you, there's generally implied consent to receive additional communications, but to be on the safe side, it's worth adding a sentence to this effect in your terms of purchase agreement. This way, if they report you for sending spam, you can prove to your email marketing service provider that they did agree to sign up for your information.

Go to **www.veganbusinessmedia.com/resources** for details on recommended email marketing service providers.

What to send out and how often
The type and frequency of email content will vary, depending on your industry and your customers, but the key—as we saw with social media marketing—is to provide valuable, interesting, engaging, and authentic content. "I offer a special-priced spa service every month, and I send out no more than two emails a month. The trick is to let people know what's new without inundating them," says Le Petite Spa's Mary Prenon.

Candle Cafe's Joy Pierson sends occasional emails to the company's large database to make special announcements such as a new book or events at the venues, while Titbits Catering's Paula Young keeps her list updated with menus and restaurant news.

Stephanie Redcross from Vegan Mainstream emphasizes the importance of testing and measuring when it comes to email marketing. "You have to get an idea of whether you get better engagement from sending out an email once a week for a month, or twice a week for a month," says Redcross.

Remember that, as with social media, email marketing is about engaging and interacting with your customers, not just broadcasting to them.

"Sometimes, we forget our size. What large corporations do and what small businesses do are *very* different," says Redcross. "A real advantage of small businesses is they can create a level of intimacy with their customers and potential clients. Instead of thinking, 'XYZ company did this, so I'll do it,' say to yourself, 'I'm a small business. How do I create a relationship? When I send out emails, how can I do my emails differently so people can engage and interact?'"

One way to determine the level of engagement of your email list is to ask them a question and ask them to respond to you, either via return email, or to join in the conversation on your social media channels or take part in a quiz. This will also give you an idea of which content generates the best response, so you can do more of it.

While you do want to "sell" in your emails, the trick is not to do so in a pushy way. It's tempting to only email information about your products and services, but this alone is unlikely to engage your list. As we saw in Chapter 6 with the example of Nicobella's Nichole Dandrea, authenticity is the key to engagement, both on social media and via email marketing. Create content, whether it's in written, audio or video format, from your heart and share your passions from a meaningful place. People will respond far more positively to you and your brand.

Branded Products

On my fridge at home I have fridge magnets for the local plumber, electrician, and other trades people. They're all in one place, easy to see, and don't disappear into the ether like business cards have a tendency to do (although you should still have a business card).

Branded items are a great way to keep your product or service top of mind. Be creative. Don't just think cups, pens, fridge magnets, and t-shirts (although those are all good). What else could you produce that will ensure your brand is memorable?

Nacheez's Ilsa Hess found an innovative way to market her vegan cheese: Car magnets. Along with free sample packs, these have proved popular with interested customers. "My car and my mother's car both have Nacheez ad magnets on the doors. Sometimes, we get people asking for the free samples while we're waiting at a red light. It's fun to launch a free sample at them through their car window!" says Hess.

Google and Other Search Engines

Some marketers say search engine optimization (SEO) is dead. And, to some degree, they're right. As we saw in Chapter 6, Google has introduced a plethora of algorithms (named after birds) that have disrupted the status quo and left many business owners reeling. Many SEO specialists hired by these business owners employed black hat (dodgy) techniques to keep their clients' websites on the front page of Google for particular search terms—often unknown to the business owner. Now that Google has clamped down on what it declares unethical practices, unsuspecting business owners have been penalized, with their long-standing websites cast way down the rankings, often by several pages. Even those businesses that pay for Google Adwords aren't getting the organic results they once did.

The good news is that Google has recognized that web content shouldn't be optimized for Google bots, but for people. This has resulted in the disappearance of a ton of spammy sites with useless content. The idea is that people should discover sites with the most relevant and highest-quality content for their search criteria. And the best way to do this is to create relevant, valuable, and engaging content for your audience on a consistent basis. This includes blogging on your business website, creating audio and video content for your social media channels, and creating content for other good-quality blogs or online magazines. This is known as **content marketing**.

Coming up in search engine results is a useful way to grow your business, particularly on a local front. It's important to optimize your website so that you appear for specific, relevant keywords.

"We can be found on Google if you type in 'humane pest control,'" says Humane Wildlife Solutions's Kevin Newell. "While we don't regard the animals that our clients call us about as pests, this is a keyword that potential customers will probably use when looking for a business to rid them of their problem. By branding ourselves under the heading of 'pest control,' we're more likely to be found by people who were not searching specifically for a solution that's humane."

Team Up With a Non-Profit (or Start Your Own)

As we saw in Chapter 4 on relationships, collaborating with a non-proft organization can help to build awareness of your brand. Donating a prize or sponsoring an event or fundraiser is a win-win situation. "We sponsor and donate to almost everyone who asks. So, if any animal charities or vegan groups are doing fundraisers, we'll always donate something and they'll put our name on their website or flyers," says The Cruelty Free Shop's Jessica Bailey.

Addiction Food is another big charity sponsor.

"Through donations and sponsorship, people will talk about your business and it can attract the attention from people with influence in the vegan and animal rights community as well," says owner Georgie Campbell.

The Vegan Proteins team Giacomo Marchese and Dani Taylor went so far as to create their own non-profit, PlantBuilt—a vegan bodybuilding organization whose mission is to demonstrate the benefits of plant-based eating in achieving success in competing in strength-based sports. Vegan Proteins sponsors PlantBuilt competitions, and the member athletes spread the word about veganism even further by inspiring and leading by example. And of course Vegan Proteins raises its profile as a sponsor.

Apps

Depending on the nature of your business and your target audience, an app is another way to get in front of your customers. As with any content, it must be relevant and valuable. Unless you're an expert in technology, you'll need to hire someone to work with you to create an app.

Be clear about what your aims are and what you hope to achieve. I've seen a few business owners who launched a free app, assuming they'd be able to finance it by selling ads on it, but this didn't happen. Others have launched a paid app, only to find their market wasn't prepared to pay even a few dollars for it and expected it for free.

Afterword
Lessons Learned

Running any kind of business is fraught with challenges. You'll make mistakes; you'll make decisions that you later regret. It's all par for the course and part of the learning process that enables you and, ultimately, your business to grow.

That said, it doesn't hurt to avoid as many pitfalls as you can, and I hope that, after being privy to the generous insights from the 65 vegan business owners, entrepreneurs, and professionals in this book, you can minimize worst-case scenarios.

It takes courage to start a business, and it can be scary at times. Running a business on vegan principles has its extra challenges. I trust that you'll take comfort and inspiration from the journeys of this book's contributors.

I asked each of the interviewees what key lessons—personal or professional—they've learned from running their businesses to date. It seems fitting to end this book with a selection of some of those responses:

Sugandh G. Agrawal, GUNAS
"Running my business has helped me expand my comfort zone. Initially, when I started out, I just wanted to hide behind my drawing board and only design bags. Now it's so much different, and I feel that, even if you're a designer, it's so important to talk about what you're doing and explain it to people. Not everybody is a designer; not everybody thinks artistically."

Jessica Bailey, The Cruelty Free Shop
"I've learned that the staff you have around you are *so* important,

and I've learned to trust other people when you're used to doing everything yourself."

Tim Barford, Yaoh and VegFestUK
"Don't take yourself seriously. When others have a go at you, make sure you see the funny side. Don't get too wrapped up around complaints. There'll always be people who'll disagree with what you're doing, and they may not like it. In the vegan community, they may feel very strongly about something and aren't afraid to express it. Always keep your sense of humor."

David Benzaquen, PlantBased Solutions
"I've learned that I am more suited to be a general practitioner than a tactician because I get more excited about developing grand visions and overall strategies to success than spending my time on any one particular area of a business. I learned very early on how easy it is to underestimate the cost that goes into providing services and covering overheads. I've learned that business doesn't have to be a four-letter word and that we can use business to change the world."

Jessica Burman, Cocoon Apothecary
"There are people out there who you can't trust. Protect yourself. Don't get discouraged. Even if things are slow, they're likely developing, and that's the right direction. Don't burn any bridges; you never know when an opportunity will come out of left field. Treat everyone you meet well. Let go of any money neurosis."

Ginger Burr, Total Image Consultants
"Believe you can do it. Only do what you love and delegate the rest. Surround yourself with people who believe in you. Follow the golden rule of treating others as you'd like to be treated. Keep good records because you never know when the tax department will come calling! Don't give everything away—this is mainly

directed at women. Charge what you're worth."

Georgie Campbell, Addiction Food
"There's no substitute for hard work. Also, I don't have time for procrastination, whether it's my own or anyone else's. I find I've lost a little bit of patience, and once I need to make a decision, I just go for it. The other important thing is to give people your trust, but not too much, and go with your gut feeling."

Pablo Castro, Dr-Cow
"You can always change your mind about things you thought were a particular way and now are different. Don't be stubborn; listen to other people's thoughts. Take your time to think and meditate."

Samantha Crosby, Ayana Organics
"I've learned, often the hard way, about self-preservation and the art of saying 'no.' I've learned about having good boundaries between work life and family life. I've learned to delegate and to have trust in other people that they can perform tasks well without me. I've also learned that you can completely change career paths with no experience of your new chosen field, and build something from scratch that you're proud of and that other people want to be involved with."

Nichole Dandrea, Nicobella
"You really learn what your strengths and weakness are. What I've learned about myself is that I need to be able to let some things go and let somebody else do it who has the ability to do it, trusting that it will get done, so I don't have to do everything."

Linda Doby, Wellinhand
"You've got to believe in yourself so others will too—enthusiasm sells."

Eva Fung, ESPE
"Be humble, listen and have an open mind. I've learned to love criticism. That means people care about making your business better."

Sharon Gannon, Jivamukti Yoga
"I've learned the importance of communication—to be very clear, speaking to your employees, your teachers, your students. Really work hard at communication skills—that's the most valuable thing I've learned; and I'm still learning."

Kendall Hayes, Iku Wholefood
"I've learned that, although I want to do everything myself, I must let go of control and delegate. I've learned that although I usually think I know best, there are thousands of people before me who learned the hard way and have wisdom to offer me. I've learned that to remain true to my beliefs, I need to surround myself with like-minded people. I've also learned that lifestyle is important and wealth is relative. There's no point working 18 hours a day to make more money if your health and family life suffer."

Swami Hennessy-Mitchell, CocoLuscious
"Having a strong vision is fundamental to achieving goals. I can't do everything on my own. It's okay to ask for help and to delegate. Having systems, procedures, and a great team are essential. Regardless of you doing what you love to do, there will still be massive challenges."

Ilsa Hess, Nacheez
"Don't take things personally. You're putting yourself out there, and it can be scary. You'll be exposed to thousands of people, and each of them have their own opinions and experiences. Many people will greet you with a smiling face and will be very polite. Some will tell you your product is horrible and you should go out of business. I've learned to ask the second set of

people why they think that way. They are the people who are honest about their opinions, and your interactions with them will help you and your business grow. Learning to thank those who are kind to you and also thank those who are mean to you first takes stepping back and taking yourself out of the equation. They aren't talking about you as a person; they're talking about your product. Not taking things personally also helps you not take on someone else who's having a bad day."

Ken Israel, Iku Wholefood
"Watch the figures. You get into a business like this because of a passion, but if you don't watch the bottom line all the time, you're out the back door."

Ele Keats, Ele Keats Jewelry
"You can't learn it all in one year. Give yourself the experience of growing. Be humble, learn to learn, and take it all in. Be open and don't allow your ego to get in the way."

Leigh-Chantelle, Viva La Vegan!
"I've learned not to trust the people who talk the most. So many people just talk and talk about what they're going to do or what they can do or how I should get involved with what they're going to do. I find I no longer have time for those people who don't actually *do* anything."

Whitney Lauritsen, Eco-Vegan Gal
"Never give up, focus on progress instead of perfection, and always keep learning."

Heather Lounsbury, Live Natural Live Well
"I learned to believe in myself and know that my purpose in wanting to help people and wanting to help animals is so important, that it's worth putting the work into every single day."

Grace Love, Bliss Organic Café
"Be flexible and embrace change. Change is good."

Clare Mann, psychologist and communications trainer
"I've learned to do my due diligence on people who want to work with me. People are attracted to bright, shiny objects and will do anything to work with people who are passionate and committed to being successful. However, while it's important to believe that everyone is capable of being ethical, it's a mistake to project your own values onto people as if theirs will be identical. So do your due diligence with an open mind, as it is a responsibility to the integrity of your business and to your existing clients. Be prepared and committed to thinking big and taking risks, knowing that if they don't work out, you have learned one more way not to do something. But try not to repeat your mistakes and learn from what works and what doesn't."

Giacomo Marchese, Vegan Proteins
"Don't be afraid to invest into your business without an immediate return on your investment. Growth takes time and resources, and the reward will be there, but you have to go after it. Be the face of your business and be transparent. Image isn't everything, and people can see right through those who choose to sell an idea or concept more so than what they actually believe in and who they are. People will relate to your human side, not something you're pretending to be. Be who you are, and others are more likely to support you in the long run, and you'll ultimately be a happier person, living by example."

Mellissa Morgan, Ms. Cupcake
"I've learned to trust my instincts and know when to say, 'We need to stop doing this.' Knowing when to quit is just as valuable as knowing when to grow."

Ella Nemcova, The Regal Vegan

"Get to know people and really develop a curiosity for the human condition because, once you learn to satisfy the needs of people in your circles, I think then you really start to get a sense of success."

Kevin Newell, Humane Wildlife Solutions

"You need to remain confident and motivated. If you're confident about your business, your product, or service, then those you speak to will have confidence in you and your business too. Staying motivated to keep going, even through tough times, is essential. You have to keep on track and keep going, and the business will flourish."

Mike Newman, Ethical Wares

"Do what you believe in, what you feel comfortable with, and don't worry too much about what others are doing. In a world full of so much cruelty and injustice, the slightest 'good' action is to be celebrated. Don't lose the ability to be humble, learn from others, and apologize when in the wrong."

Tracie O'Keefe, hypnotherapist, naturopath, and business mindset coach

"There are people who make it their mission to bring you down, especially if you're what they consider to be too weird or different. I've learned to be resilient and not allow the negativity of others to prevent me from following my passions and doing work that I love."

Elizabeth Olsen, Olsenhaus

"Only open a business in a field you're an expert in and have worked for large- and small-scale companies in that industry. Have savings of at least two years and know that you will spend more time and money than you have planned. Keep your ego in check and always remember why you created the business in the first place. Know that people will copy and steal your name, your look, your product. Address the issue with a letter from a lawyer and move forward, but, by the time someone is copying all of your things, you should have already moved onto the next thing."

Rudy Penando, Vx
"Customers aren't always right, but when they are right, you need to think about it and adjust."

Tracy Perkins, Strawberry Hedgehog
"Learning to take feedback constructively, even when it's not presented in the gentlest manner, is the best lesson I have learned. Every interaction and challenge is an opportunity to learn more about your business, more about yourself, or about letting go. Being open to change and rolling with the punches are essential for any business, and life, for that matter."

Joy Pierson, Candle Cafe
"Stay grounded, be loving, always keep a positive attitude, and use positive language. Make it fun and celebrate every day, no matter what you're doing. Whether I'm doing dishes or entertaining a celebrity at the restaurant, there's no difference; I celebrate it all."

Bart Potenza, Candle Cafe
"The healthier and stronger we are, the more exciting we make our endeavors, and people pick up on that and are attracted to it."

Mary Prenon, Le Petite Spa
"Most of my mistakes were picking the wrong place to advertise. Start with something small, such as a local newspaper, or a small budget for Facebook ads. Then see how they're working before you decide to commit to something more expensive."

Renia Pruchnicki, Truth Belts

"Have a bit of humility and let go of your ego, of this being your baby, and let other people come in to help you. Don't be offended if somebody suggests something for you."

Stephanie Redcross, Vegan Mainstream

"I realized that my dream was one thing but maybe that wasn't the road, so I've had to tweak my services over the years and offer them a little bit differently. I had to test different pricing structures and so forth. Sometimes, frustration can set in when you think the dream is *this*, and *this* is the finish line, and you imagine there's only one way to get there. But the reality is there are many ways. You have to be flexible, have faith, and stay motivated so that when bad stuff happens, you can deal with it as part of regular life and business. You have to shake it off or have a support system in place that can help you put things into perspective."

Amanda Solomons, Rubyfruit

"Be authentic. People respond to authenticity and passion. Be true to yourself. Be flexible and adaptive, but don't compromise on your values, and people will respect that. Recognize what you don't know, and ask for help when you need it. Be kind. Focus on your own business—don't compare yourself to others. Be generous, even when you have little money. Oh, and don't respond to internet trolls!"

Dani Taylor, Vegan Proteins

"I've learned that I am so much more capable than I thought I was. I had been letting fear hold me back quite a bit. This is one of my biggest weaknesses. I've learned that you can be just as scared to succeed as you are to fail. I've learned that working with someone with completely different strengths than you is probably the best thing you could ever do, although it's definitely challenging. When you work with someone whose brain works differently than yours, you open your endeavors up to completely new heights. I've learned to have a thicker skin. The more successful you become, the more in the public eye you are, and everyone is a critic. You can't let it get to you. You can't please everyone all the time."

Lagusta Yearwood, Lagusta's Luscious
"Trust yourself above all others. Have patience and compassion for others. It took me a while to learn that doing something for short-term profit that wasn't helpful for the long-term health of the business was a mistake. We used to say 'yes' to every whole-sale order and special order that came our way, but I've learned that sometimes saying 'no' can be a stronger choice."

Paula Young, Titbits Catering
"Always be open to new opportunities. Every conversation you have could lead to potential customers or business opportunities. Not everything in life goes as planned. There are bound to be some low points, but there are always more highs. I take each day as it comes and always try to have a positive outlook."

References

Introduction

Clarkson, D. (2014, November 28). Business and entrepreneurs seize opportunities in rise of veganism. *The Guardian.* Retrieved from http://www.theguardian.com/sustainable-business/2014/nov/28/business-and-entrepreneurs-seize-opportunities-in-rise-of-veganism

Guilmet, A. (2015). Cruelty-free luxury is not an oxymoron. *Fortune.* Retrieved from http://fortune.com/2015/01/12/vegan-cruelty-free-luxury/

Holland, C. (2014, November 17). Vegan cheese company wins big on Shark Tank. *VegNews.* Retrieved from http://veg-news.com/articles/page.do?pageId=6588&catId=1

Khomami, N. (2015, February 7). From Beyoncé to the BAFTAs, vegan culture gets star status. *The Guardian.* Retrieved from http://www.theguardian.com/lifeandstyle/2015/feb/08/veganism-celebrities-baftas-beyonce-health-animal-welfare

Li, S. (2015, February 4). Vegan fashion grows more fashionable as textile technology improves. *Los Angeles Times.* Retrieved from http://www.latimes.com/business/la-fi-vegan-fashion-20150205-story.html#page=1

Lorenz, T. (2015, February 3). Beyoncé launches an on-demand vegan meal delivery service. *Business Insider Australia.* Retrieved from http://www.businessinsider.com.au/beyonce-22-days-nutrition-on-demand-vegan-meal-delivery-service-2015-2

Rami, T. (2014, January 12). Veganism in seven decades. *New York Magazine*. Retrieved from http://nymag.com/news/intelligencer/vegan-celebrities-2014-1

Stump, S. (2014). TODAY puts 'meatless' meat to the test: Does it taste like chicken? *TODAY Food*. Retrieved from http://www.today.com/food/today-puts-meatless-meat-test-does-it-taste-chicken-1D79579619

Chapter 1: Define Your Purpose

Sinek, S. (2009, September). How great leaders inspire action. *TED talk*. Retrieved from https://www.ted.com/talks/simon_sinek_how_great_leaders_inspire_action/transcript?language=en

Chapter 4: Relationships

Goldensohn, R. (2015, February 4). Vegans send 'love mail' to restaurant attacked by 'crossfit people.' *DNAinfo New York*. Retrieved from http://www.dnainfo.com/new-york/20150204/chelsea/vegans-send-love-mail-restaurant-attacked-by-crossfit-people

Chapter 9: PR and Media

Fallon, N. (2014, August 14). How to Respond to a HARO Query. *LinkedIn Pulse*. Retrieved from https://www.linkedin.com/pulse/20140814213820-80904433-how-to-respond-to-a-haro-query

Resources

Books

Personal Development

Awaken the Giant Within: How to Take Immediate Control of Your Mental, Emotional, Physical and Financial Destiny!
by Anthony Robbins

Communicate: How to Say What Needs to Be Said, When It Needs to Be Said, in the Way It Needs to Be Said
by Clare Mann

Fearless Living: Live Without Excuses and Love Without Regret
by Rhonda Britten

Feel the Fear and Do It Anyway
by Susan Jeffers

Flow: The Psychology of Happiness
by Mihaly Csikszentmihalyi

How to Be an Adult in Relationships: The Five Keys to Mindful Loving
by David Richo

How to Make Love All the Time: Make Love Last a Lifetime
by Barbara DeAngelis

Inspiration for Survive and Prosper: Personal Transformation Out of Crisis
by Tracie O'Keefe

Man's Search for Meaning
by Viktor Frankl

Radical Forgiveness
by Colin Tipping

Take the Next Step: Secrets to Creating Success and Manifesting Your Dreams
by Mai Lieu

There is Nothing Wrong With You: Going Beyond Self-Hate
by Cheri Huber

The Gifts of Imperfection: Let Go of Who You Think You're Supposed to Be and Embrace Who You Are
by Brené Brown

The Law of Divine Compensation: On Work, Money & Miracles
by Marianne Williamson

The Me Myth: What Do You Mean It's Not All About Me?
by Andrew Griffiths

The Path to Love: Spiritual Lessons for Creating the Love You Need
by Deepak Chopra

The Places that Scare You: A Guide to Fearlessness
by Pema Chodron

The Power of Now: A Guide to Spiritual Enlightenment
by Eckhart Tolle

The Secret of the Shadow
by Debbie Ford

The Values Factor: The Secret to Creating an Inspired and Fulfilling Life
by John Demartini

Welcome to Your Life: Simple Insights For Your Inspiration and Empowerment
by Ronny K. Prasad

Wishes Fulfilled: Mastering the Art of Manifesting
by Wayne Dyer

Business, Marketing and Selling

Book Yourself Solid: The Fastest, Easiest, and Most Reliable System for Getting More Clients Than You Can Handle Even if You Hate Marketing and Selling
by Michael Port

The E-Myth Revisited: Why Most Small Businesses Don't Work and What to Do About It
by Michael E. Gerber

Guerrilla Marketing Goes Green: Winning Strategies to Improve Your Profits and Your Planet
by Jay Conrad Levinson and Shel Horowitz

How to Win Friends and Influence People
by Dale Carnegie

Influence: The Psychology of Persuasion
by Robert Cialdini

Made to Stick: Why Some Ideas Survive and Others Die
by Chip Heath and Dan Heath

Permission Marketing: Turning Strangers into Friends and Friends into Customers
by Seth Godin

Pitch Anything: An Innovative Method for Presenting, Persuading, and Winning the Deal
by Oren Klaff

Power Stories: The 8 Stories You Must Tell to Build an Epic Business
by Valerie Khoo

Purple Cow: Transform Your Business by Being Remarkable
by Seth Godin

Shark Tank: Jump Start Your Business
by Michael Parrish DuDell

The 7 Habits of Highly Effective People
by Steven R. Covey

The $100 Start Up: Fire Your Boss, Do What You Love and Work Better to Live More
by Chris Guillebeau

Unconscious Branding: How Neuroscience Can Empower (and Inspire) Marketing
by Douglas Van Praet

Yes! Energy: The Equation to Do Less, Make More
by Loral Langemeier

Online

Vegan Business Media
www.veganbusinessmedia.com

Country-Specific Business Resources

US

Small Business Administration
www.sba.gov

Internal Revenue Service
www.irs.gov

Canada

Canada Business Network
www.canadabusiness.ca

Australia

Australian Government: Business
www.business.gov.au

Australian Taxation Office
www.ato.gov.au

UK
Gov.uk
www.gov.uk

List of Interviewees

The following business owners, listed in alphabetical order, kindly shared their insights into how to start and grow a successful vegan enterprise.

Sugandh G. Agrawal
GUNAS (US)
www.gunasthebrand.com

Sandy Anderson
Veganpet (AU)
www.veganpet.com.au

Ben Asamani
222 Veggie Vegan (UK)
www.222veggievegan.com

Jessica Bailey
The Cruelty Free Shop (AU)
www.crueltyfreeshop.com.au

Tim Barford
Yaoh and **VegFestUK** (UK)
www.yaoh.co.uk
www.vegfest.co.uk

Kendall Hayes
Iku Wholefood (AU)
www.ikuwholefood.com.au
www.naturallykendall.com

Simone Bateman and
Amanda Solomons
Rubyfruit (AU)
www.facebook.com/
rubyfruitveganbakery

David Benzaquen
PlantBased Solutions (US)
www.plantbasedsolutions.com

Jessica Burman
Cocoon Apothecary (CA)
www.cocoonapothecary.com

Ginger Burr
Total Image Consultants (US)
www.totalimageconsultants.com

Georgie Campbell and
Grant Campbell
Addiction Food (AU)
www.addictionfood.com.au

Pablo Castro
Dr-Cow (US)
www.dr-cow.com

Lee Coates
Cruelty Free Super (AU) and
Ethical Investors (UK)
www.crueltyfreesuper.com.au
www.ethicalinvestors.co.uk

Samantha Crosby
Ayana Organics (AU)
www.ayanaorganics.com.au

Nichole Dandrea
Nicobella Organics (US)
www.nicobellaorganics.com

Melissa Dion
Ecolissa (US)
www.Ecolissa.com

Linda Doby
Wellinhand (US)
www.wellinhand.com

JL Fields
JL Fields Consulting, LLC (US)
www.jlfieldsconsulting.com
www.jlgoesvegan.com

Wally Fry
Fry's Family Foods (AU)
www.frysinternational.com

Eva Fung
ESPE (CA)
www.espe.ca

Sharon Gannon
Jivamukti Yoga (US)
www.jivamuktiyoga.com

Swami Hennessy-Mitchell
CocoLuscious (AU)
www.cocoluscious.com.au

Ilsa Hess
Nacheez (US)
www.nacheez.com

Ken Israel
Iku Wholefood (AU)
www.ikuwholefood.com.au

Kezia Jauron
Evolotus PR (US)
www.evolotuspr.com

Jeremy Johnson
Vegan Perfection (AU)
www.veganperfection.com.au

Ele Keats
Ele Keats Jewelry (US)
www.elekeats.com

Sara Kidd
Freelance Branding Consultant (AU)
www.sarakidd.com

Alicia Lai
Bourgeois Boheme (UK)
www.bboheme.com

Whitney Lauritsen
Eco-Vegan Gal (US)
www.ecovegangal.com

Leigh-Chantelle
Epicentre Equilibrium and **Viva La Vegan!** (AU)
www.leigh-chantelle.com
www.vivalavegan.com

Loren Lembke
Bounty Burgers (AU)
www.facebook.com/
BountyBurgers

Eric Lindstrom
ThankTank Creative (US)
www.thanktankcreative.com

Adrian Ling
Plamil Foods (UK)
www.plamilfoods.co.uk

Heather Lounsbury
Live Natural Live Well (US)
www.livenaturallivewell.com

Grace Love
Bliss Organic Café (AU)
www.blissorganiccafe.com.au

Clare Mann
Communicate 31 (AU)
www.communicate31.com
www.claremann.com

Giacomo Marchese and
Dani Taylor
Vegan Proteins (US)
www.veganproteins.com

Justin Mead
Vegan Style (AU) and
Zette Shoes (AU)
www.veganstyle.com.au
www.zetteshoes.com

Nikki Medwell
Bed and Broccoli (AU)
www.bedandbroccoli.com.au

Victoria Moran
Main Street Vegan Academy (US)
www.mainstreetvegan.net

Mellissa Morgan
Ms. Cupcake (UK)
www.mscupcake.co.uk

Ella Nemcova
The Regal Vegan (US)
www.theregalvegan.com

Kevin Newell
Humane Wildlife Solutions (UK)
www.humanewildlifesolu-tions.co.uk

Mike Newman
Ethical Wares (UK)
www.ethicalwares.com

Donna Oakes-Jones
Cow Jones Industrials (US)
www.cowjonesindustrials.com

Tracie O'Keefe
O'Keefe & Fox Industries Pty Ltd (AU)
www.tracieokeefe.com
www.doctorok.com

Elizabeth Olsen
Olsenhaus (US)
www.olsenhaus.com

Rudy Penando
Vx (UK)
www.vegancross.com

Tracy Perkins
Strawberry Hedgehog (US)
www.strawberryhedgehog.com

T.K. Pillan
Veggie Grill (US)
www.veggiegrill.com

Joy Pierson and Bart Potenza
Candle Cafe, Candle Cafe West and Candle 79 (US)
www.candlecafe.com
www.candlecafe.com/west
www.candle79.com

Ron Prasad
Impetus Success Australia (AU)
www.impetussuccess.com.au

Mary Prenon
Le Petite Spa (US)
www.lepetitespany.com

Renia Pruchnicki
Truth Belts (CA)
www.truthbelts.com

Stephanie Redcross
Vegan Mainstream (US)
www.veganmainstream.com

Karin Ridgers
Mad Promotions and
VeggieVision TV (UK)
www.mad-promotions.com
www.veggievision.tv

Seth Tibbott
Tofurky (US)
www.tofurky.com

Jane Velez-Mitchell
Jane Unchained (US)
www.janeunchained.com

Lagusta Yearwood
Lagusta's Luscious (US)
www.lagustasluscious.com

Paula Young
Titbits Catering (UK)
www.titbitscatering.co.uk

Advertisements

The businesses whose advertisements appear on the following pages are sponsor partners of this book. They are all owned and operated by passionate, committed ethical vegans.

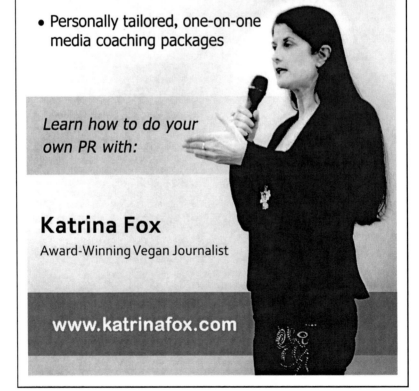

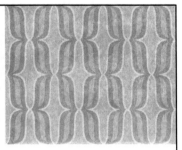

CPSIA information can be obtained at www.ICGtesting.com
Printed in the USA
LVOW10s0046230216

476295LV00026B/241/P